Black Dragon
Ch'i Kung

Sifu Tony Salvitti

"Without going out the door, know the world.

Without peering out the window, see the Heavenly Tao.

The further one goes
The less one knows.

Therefore the sage
Knows without going,
Names without seeing,
Achieves without striving.

Those who pursue the knowledge, increase every day.

Those who pursue Tao, decrease every day."

— Lao Tzu

Contents

Introduction to your new life~~~~~~8

The first step~~~~~~15

Learning to move~~~~~~18

Drinking and eating~~~~~~19

Discipline and desire~~~~~~20

Herb's for health~~~~~~23

The three treasure's~~~~~~99

Cultivating ch'i into jing~~~~~~154

Taoist longevity secrets~~~~~~166

Black Dragon Ch'i Kung~~~~~~209

Introduction to your new life

The concept of Ch'i, is really a simple one. Often people oversimplify or make it too esoteric to understand or relate to the layman. Ch'i is also called "Ki" in Japanese, "Prana" in ancient Sanskrit and modern yoga, "Vital force" in English, "Huna" in the Polynesian cultures, and in over 97 other cultures around the world.

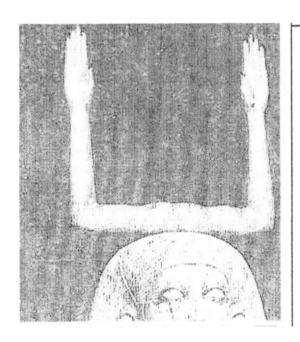

The hieroglyph *Ka* (the root word for work, specifically *lifting* or *carrying*), mounted on the head of King Horus, denotes the force that created and preserved life, and ultimately gathers it up in death. *Ka* is believed to have originally meant "that physical power that set objects in motion."
From Painting, Sculpture and Architecture of Ancient Egypt *by Wolfhart Westendorf.*

The ancient Egyptian concept of "Ka" is identical to the Chinese "Ch'i". In ancient Hebrew it is "Ruach" ,the ancient Greeks called it "Pneuma", and our word *spirit*, from the Latin *spiritus*.

It is the life force that is in every living thing and flow's in, around and threw all inanimate objects. The fact of the matter is for the younger generation (after George Lucas Star Wars movie) is that he took a majority of his "The Force" concept from Asian martial arts and even the design of "Darth Vader's" helmet was from the ancient Japanese Samurai battle helmet. If you replaced the "light sabers" with Samurai sword's you would have a excellent medieval martial arts movie.

To give him credit with this movie and book which is excellent Along with "Master Yoda". Who sites many ancient ch'i kung quotes that are in essence very valid and well worded for modern times.

"Always pass on what you have learned.", "Train yourself to let go of everything you fear to lose.", "Powerful you have become, the dark side I sense in you.", "PATIENCE YOU MUST HAVE.", "You will know (the good from the bad) when you are calm, at peace. Passive. A Jedi uses the Force for knowledge and defense, never for attack.", "Fear is the path to the dark side. Fear leads to anger. Anger leads to hate. Hate leads to suffering.", "Feel the force!", "You must unlearn what you have learned.", "When you look at the dark side, careful you must be. For the dark side looks back.", "Do or do not. There is no try.", "May the Force be with you.", "Size matters not. Look at me. Judge me by my size, do you? Hmm? Hmm. And well you should not. For my ally is the Force, and a powerful ally it is. Life creates it, makes it grow. Its energy surrounds us and binds us. Luminous beings are we, not this crude matter. You must feel the Force around you; here, between you, me, the tree, the rock, everywhere, yes. Even between the land and the ship.", "Named must your fear be before banish it you can."

All of the Yoda quotes are good and can be used in everyday life. They can help people relate and are so valid in fact a whole religious movement is based on "Jedi training" in Australia.

Once you start down the path of learning to get in touch with your body (down to every last cell). Increase the amount of ch'i (Qi) in your body, then cultivate it (over time) and eventually learn to harness it and project this life force to heal other people, animals, even plants. Or if need be use it for self defense purposes-never to attack.

You should develop a sense to learn something each and everyday. Just from daily practice of the basic's (breathing, concentration, stances,etc.) you will open up a deeper understanding of yourself, your body, and your environment.

Having started off early in the "yang" or hard/external martial arts. I gave no credence what so ever to the "yin" or soft/internal martial arts. Like;Tai ch'i chuan, Hisng-i, Xin yi quan, or even the Japanese Aikido. I thought that to be the most powerful (my goal at the time) amounted to muscle strength, speed, and stamina, combined with leverage and knowledge of anatomy.

However, I was totally wrong and nothing further from the truth. I was training in Virginia under a Tae Kwon Do master named Kim. I along with a few of my friends (2 Marines and one Navy) were invited to a Chinese master's kwoon (training hall) to witness a demonstration of Black Dragon Xin yi quan an internal martial art.

After arriving we witnessed the usual throwing around students and catching blocks and kicks. Then Master Kwan's wife who was barley weighing one hundred pounds and five feet two inches (if that).

Master Kwan asked if anyone of us could take her down? I volunteered and once again "thought" I was going to take it easy on this old lady. Just sweep her back and pin her on her back. I made my move and before I could grab her she landed a double palm strike to my chest and I was flying backwards three to five feet and landed on my ass!

I could not understand or believe how this small woman could have done that and the other weird thing was she did not even seem affected by her winning the fight with me. She just laughed and smiled.

When she hit my chest it did not feel like a normal painful punch or slap. Instead The only way I could describe it at the time was like I floated away from her. It was effortless for her and I never felt anything like this before.

Needless to say I was intrigued by the internal "yin" kung fu. Later on after many years of training under Master Kwan Li, I came to understand the concept, development of ch'i kung (Qi Gong), and now knew that while people 'seem' to be weak or frail doing slow repetitive Tai ch'i chuan, Xin yi quan or other internal martial art. They take longer to learn but will be more powerful and are in fact superior to all external martial arts.

This is because the longer a individual practices ch'i kung (for ease or not listing all internal arts) the more ch'i strength (force) they will have. It is the opposite of muscular strength that will fade as one gets older. With Ch'i strength you get even more stronger and more powerful.

Lao Kun (ch'i power from the palms)

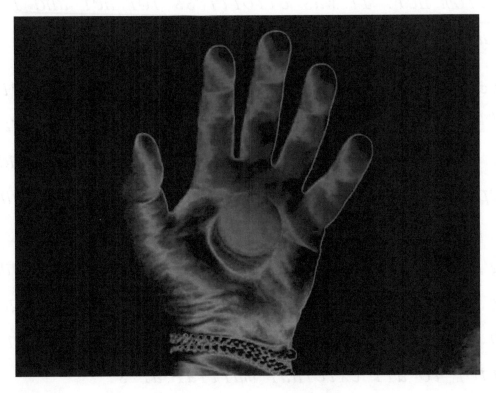

Ch'i projected from the "Lao kun" chakra, can be used to heal (as in laying on of hands) , and in the healing side of martial arts or to repel for defense.

The first step

Ch'i Kung, sometimes written as "Qi Gong", is an integrative practice of breathing excercises, body postures and/or visualizations designed to cultivate life energy and circulate it through the body. Ch'i, or "Ki" (Japanese), can be translated as "life force" and kung as "accomplishment or skill." The main goal of ch'i kung practice is to improve and maintain health. However, other purposes include spiritual practice and martial arts training. For the Taoist practitioner, ch'i kung supports the nourishment of mind, body and spirit.

Tao is the Term used in ancient Chinese religious philosophy, signifying "the Way" or pathway of life. The Tao is understood as a unity underlying the opposites and diversity of the phenomenal world. Ching Shen Li (cosmic energy) is manifest in the duality of yin and yang (negative and positive), female and male principles in nature.

Yin and yang are also energies in the individual human body and the balancing of these energies is one of the tasks of life. The correct harmony between yin and yang may be achieved through diet, **meditation,** and a life of truth, simplicity, and tranquility, identifying with the Tao of nature.

This is the union with the law of the universe through wisdom and detached action. Special techniques of Taoist **yoga** normalize and enhance the flow of vital energy in the human body. This yoga is variously named K'ai-men (open door), *Ho-Ping* (unity), and *Ho-Hsieh* (harmony). *K'ai-Men* implies opening the path to the channels of mind, spirit, and body so that they reflect the balance of yin and yang and a harmony with the energy of the cosmos.

Taoist yoga is very similar to the **kundalini** yoga systems of ancient India, and it is not clear whether such a parallel system originated by direct influence of traveling mystics or by spontaneous rediscovery of basic truths.

Both Indian and Chinese yogas are concerned with the control of vital energy, seen as the force behind sexual activity, but which may be diverted into different channels in the body for blissful expansion of consciousness. For centuries the techniques of Chinese yoga were little known in the West; teaching manuals were closely guarded and not translated into Western languages. Teachings were usually transmitted orally from teacher to pupil.

The original Black Dragon Scroll

Learning to move

Taoists employ several different methods of meditation. The simplest form, and the most similar to the Buddhist and Hindu traditions, is the inner alchemical meditation. The goal of this meditation is to calm and empty the mind and circulate chi. Like many other practices, Taoist meditation can incorporate mantras, such as repeating the word "om," or focusing on an object or a sound, or simply focusing on the breath. While meditating, you may sit cross legged, in a chair, lie down or even walk. A Taoist may also use visualization techniques in meditation. For example a practitioner may visualize anything from simple energy moving through the body to growing up from a small child to the current adult state. When practicing ch'i kung do so during calm weather outside and during foul weather preferably indoors.

Drinking and eating

Taoists strive to live by the principles of harmony with nature and balance in everyday life. Diet plays and important role in achieving this goal. The Taoist diet is one of simplicity, focusing on whole foods that are easy digest. Avoiding chemicals and processed foods is also important. Although historically, some Taoists avoided eating grain, it is now considered a healthy part of a Taoist diet if eaten in moderation. Eating gently cooked, warm, seasonal whole foods help keep the body and mind in balance and harmony. Moderation is emphasized in the Taoist diet(about 3 ounces or less per meal), however, there are foods that are typically avoided such as meats, especially red meats, dairy, citrus fruits and spicy or acidic foods. Wheat and other "grains" are also avoided.

Discipline and desire

In able to understand the Taoist's way of thinking, one must first understand the underlying concepts of Taoism and from there learn to apply it. Anyone that has read the Tao will say that the book is extremely simple.

The writing is simple, the language is simple, and the themes are simple. The **Tao Te Ching** uses nature to express this simplicity, an extremely important theme of Taoism. The Tao describes how, like nature, one should be in balance, harmony, and simple. Verse 37 of the Tao Te Ching quotes: "People would be content with their simple, everyday lives, in harmony, and free of desire. When there is no desire, all things are at peace". Like Buddhist's beliefs, Taoism also emphasizes how desire complicates people's daily lives. Desire complicates actions that are taken and contaminate our minds. This complexity should be replaced by simplicity so that we may be more content.

When values such as, balance, harmony, and simplicity are met, they guide us to live a life of integrity. By living in such a way, we learn to be an exceptional ruler, teacher, or being. For example, verse 17 explains what a great ruler should be like. According to the Tao, the greatest leaders are those that are unknown to their subjects. The leader should organize matter in harmony with the Tao, and the subjects will go about their daily work. In the end the people will say "Amazing: we did it, all by ourselves!" By being in harmony, the leader is also able to trust his subjects more. The Tao says "if you do not trust the people, you make them untrustworthy." Having both party's content is what makes a leader exceptional.

Along with simplicity, Taoism also teaches nothingness and emptiness through the concept of wu wei. Wu is defined as 'not' or 'without.' Wei is then defined as "to do, to make, or to cause"

Literally translating the meaning of the two words is 'acting upon something.' In Taoism, the phrase **wu wei** (woo whee) can be interpreted as meaning 'to act but not to possess the act.' The meaning of not possessing the act is simply that one should not be attached to the outcome of the action. One should simply just act, not thinking of what that action will bring to them. "It means to follow the flow of nature, without trying. Rather than constantly trying to fight situations and control them, which is unnatural and self-defeating, it is better to understand the true nature of the Tao, behaving completely naturally and in tune with the natural order of things"

Herb's for health

Chinese herbs have served as the foundation for "Traditional Chinese Medicine", or TCM, for over 5,000 years. The fundamental idea of living in harmony with nature and the environment forms the basis for the use of Chinese herbs as well as the traditional Chinese approach to health. Knowledge of the healing power of Chinese herbs and herbal remedies has been passed down from generation to generation, and today represents one of China's greatest gifts to mankind.

The isolation of China throughout history plays a role in the general lack of understanding about Chinese herbs by other world civilizations. However, since the opening of China in 1972, knowledge of the ancient healing powers of Chinese herbs has been gradually spreading to western countries.

Chinese herbs are now experiencing a rapid increase in usage and popularity.

Health-conscious consumers are concerned about the concentration of synthetic chemicals in western diets, medicines, and the general environment.

Chinese herbs are being welcomed by progressive western consumers who are seeking natural, healthy and balanced alternative remedies.

Traditional Chinese Medicine is very different from the western scientific approach we are accustomed to. Chinese medical experts promote a healthful balance of yin and yang – two forces present in all of nature. When yin or yang forces or ch'i/energy levels are off-balance in the body and spirit, health problems arise. Chinese herbs and herbal remedies are used to help realign an individual's yin or yang balance in order to improve overall well-being. Chinese herbal formulas include hundreds of popular organic ingredients that work in harmony to produce the desired effects in a person's body.

These ingredients are primarily of plant origin, and may include roots, bark, seeds, flowers and leaves. Each organic ingredient typically has unique characteristics (the yin/yang balancing, ch'i/energy boosting, etc.) that are reinforced and harmonized in comprehensive ancient Chinese herbal formulas that have been passed down through the years.

For each formula sold at Chinese Herbs Direct, we provide a brief description of the formula itself and its typical actions, as well as a listing of the formula's herbal ingredients and their unique characteristics.

The study of Chinese herbs centers on the proposition that many organic substances have curative powers. Indeed, this is a fundamental tenet of not just Chinese medicine, but Western medicine as well. Popular Western remedies ranging from common aspirin to modern chemotherapy treatments have their roots in organic substances. Western medicine is finally beginning to acknowledge its debt to Chinese herbal medicine, noting that the effectiveness of many modern pharmaceuticals was originally demonstrated in Chinese herbal practice centuries ago. Nonetheless, Chinese herbs should be viewed only as a supplement to western medicine, and not as a replacement.

Chinese medicine emphasizes harmony and duality, and this is well-represented by the increasing cooperation between practitioners of Traditional Chinese Medicine and their counterparts in the western medical establishment.

In Traditional Chinese Medicine, there are roughly 13,000 medicinals used in China and over 100,000 medicinal recipes recorded in the ancient literature. Plant elements and extracts are the most common elements used in medicines- 442 were plant parts, 45 were animal parts, and 30 were minerals.

Herbal medicine, as used in Traditional Chinese Medicine (TCM), came to widespread attention in the United States in the 1970s.

In Japan, the use of TCM herbs and herbal formulas is traditionally known as "Kampo", literally "Han Chinese Medical Formulas". Many Kampo combinations are manufactured in Japan on a large scale by reputable manufacturers.

In Korea, more than 5000 herbs and 7000 herbal formulas are used in Traditional Korean Medicine for the prevention and treatment of ailments. Herbal medicine is held in great regard in North Korea, there it is known as **Tonguihak**.These are herbs and formulas that are traditionally Korean or derived from, or are used in TCM.

In Vietnam, traditional medicine comprises Thuoc Bac (Northern Medicine) and Thuoc Nam (Southern Medicine). Only those who can understand Chinese characters could diagnose and prescribe remedies in Northern Medicine.

The theory of Northern Medicine is based on the Yin-Yang interactions and the eight trigrams, as used in Chinese Medicine. Herbs such as Gleditsia are used in both Traditional Vietnamese Medicine and TCM.

Herbal medicine is held in great regard in North Korea, there it is known as **Tonguihak**.

You should always "cycle" herb's in order to provide a fresh and more potent use of them for

maximum effectiveness. Otherwise for the same effect
you will have to keep increasing the dosage over
time. Or another good method is to just abstain from
all of the herb's use for 2-3 weeks and then resume
taking the herb again.

~Asian,Ayurvedic, European, and Native American herb's~

Agrimony

Scientific Name: Agrimonia eupatoria

Common Names: Common agrimony, church steeples or sticklewort

Family:Rosaceae

Part Used:Aerial parts

Habitat:Agrimony is native to Europe, but can also be found in temperate climate in most parts of the Northern hemisphere.

Agrimony tea is soothing and good for sore throats. It is sometimes used by singers to gargle with. This herb is used to refresh and clear the throat. Agrimony is sometimes used for loose bowels as well. This herb is sometimes prescribed for fevers, digestive and bowel troubles, coughs and asthma. It can be used externally for skin sores.

CAUTION: This herb may make the skin more sensitive to sunlight and may increase the risk of sunburn. Do not take if pregnant or nursing or if you are planning to have surgery within two weeks.

Alfalfa

Scientific Name: Medicago sativa

Common Names:Buffalo grass, chilean clover, lucerne

Family:Fabaceae

Part Used:Leaves, stems, sprouts

Habitat:Alfalfa is native to southwestern Asia and Southeastern Europe. Also grows in North America and North Africa.

Alfalfa is known as the "Father of all foods" for good reason. It's loaded with important vitamins, minerals, trace minerals and protein. It's roots go down as far as 30 feet to pull valuable nutrients from the earth. This plant is commonly used for arthritis, digestive problems, as a diuretic and for reducing high cholesterol. It's a very inexpensive source of easily digested nutrients. Alfalfa is high in beta-carotene and builds the immune system. This plant also contains chlorophyll, which is good for reducing bad breath and body odor.

CAUTION: Pregnant and nursing women should not eat alfalfa seeds due to their content of stachydrine and homostachydrine (may promote menstruation or cause miscarriage). People in general should never eat alfalfa seeds. They contain high levels of the toxic amino acid canavanine. Alfalfa is high in vitamin K and may work as an anti-coagulant so it shouldn't be taken by people taking blood thinning medication.

Aloe

Scientific Name: Aloe vera

Common Names:Aloe, cape, barbados

Family:Asphodelaceae

Part Used:Leaves

Habitat:Aloe is native to the Mediterranean. It also grows in Latin America and the Caribbean.

The gel inside of the leaves of the Aloe plant can be used externally to treat minor burns, sun burn, cuts, scrapes and poison ivy. Aloe gel is good for moisturizing the skin and is a main ingredient of many skin care products. Many people use it to reduce acne and treat other skin problems.

CAUTION: Some people have taken Aloe internally as a laxative. The Mayo Clinic website states that this is not safe and can lead to severe cramping, diarrhea and dangerous imbalances of electrolytes even if used infrequently.

American Ginseng

Scientific Name: Panax quinquefolius

Common Names:Ginseng, xi yang shen

Family:Araliaceae

Part Used:Root

Habitat:American Ginseng grows in the eastern part of North America and Canada.

American ginseng is an adaptogen. An adaptogen is a substance which is good for the body in general and protects against stress of all types. This type of ginseng has been used to strengthen the immune system, increase strength and stamina, treat digestive disorders, treat diabetes, treat ADHD and as a general tonic for wellness. Many people believe that the best American ginseng comes from the state of Wisconsin in the U.S. American ginseng is considered a cooling ginseng, where Korean ginseng has a more warming effect on the body.

CAUTION: American Ginseng should not be taken by people with high blood pressure or by women who are pregnant.

Amla

Scientific Name: Phyllanthus emblica

Common Names:Indian gooseberry

Family:Phyllanthaceae

Part Used:Fruit

Habitat:Amla is native to India

Amla is often used in the Ayurvedic medicine system of India. It is rich in vitamin C and also contains many other vitamins, minerals and antioxidants. Amla is often used to treat inflammation of the joints, fevers, urinary tract infections and to control blood sugar. It is high in fiber and may be helpful in treating constipation.

Angelica

Scientific Name: Angelica archangelica

Common Names:Garden angelica, norwegian angelica, holy ghost, wild celery, masterwort

Family:Apiacae

Part Used:Leaves, stems, seeds, roots

Habitat:Angelica grows in Asia, Europe and the eastern U.S.

Angelica has traditionally been used for menopausal troubles, flatulence, appetite loss, digestive problems, respiratory ailments and arthritis. Like it's Chinese counterpart Angelica sinensis (dong quai), this herb is used by many women for the reproductive system. It is believed to be a hormonal regulator and uterine tonic. Angelica tea is often used to treat PMS as well.

CAUTION: Angelica is not recommended during pregnancy.

Anise

Scientific Name: Pimpinella anisum
Common Names:Anise
Family:Umbelliferae
Part Used:Seeds
Habitat:Anise is native to Egypt

Anise tea is made from the plant's seeds. Is has a strong licorice taste. Anise is consumed to improve digestion, prevent flatulence, reduce bad breath and to treat coughs.

Arnica

Scientific Name: Arnica montana

Common Names:Leopard's bane, mountain daisy, mountain arnica

Family:Asteraceae

Part Used:Flowers

Habitat:Arnica is native to central Asia, Siberia and Europe. Cultivated in North America.

Arnica is used externally as an ointment for sore muscles, sprains and bruises. It possesses anti-inflammatory, analgesic and anti-septic properties.

CAUTION: Arnica should never be taken internally. Not recommended for long term use as it may cause skin irritation.

Ashwagandha

Scientific Name: Withania Somnifera

Common Names:Winter cherry, indian ginseng, ajagandha

Family:Solanaceae

Part Used:Roots, leaves, seeds

Habitat:Ashwagandha grows in India, Africa and widely cultivated around the world

Ashwagandha is sometimes called "Indian ginseng" as it has many similar health properties. This herb is very popular in the Ayurvedic system of health in India. It is considered an adaptogen. It is commonly used to relieve stress and strengthen the immune system. It has the ability to strengthen the body and increase endurance. This herb has been used in India for over 3,000 years as a rejuvenator. The seeds of this plant are thought to have a diuretic effect, while the leaves possess anti-inflammatory, analgesic and sedative properties. The chemical components of the root have anti-microbial, anti-inflammatory, analgesic, immune strengthening and sedative properties. This is a great herb for athletes and active people that need to increase their energy, strength and stamina.

CAUTION: Ashwagandha is high iron content and should NEVER be taken by women during pregnancy. This herb may also have a mild depressant effect and should not be taken with sedatives or alcohol.

Astragalus

Scientific Name: Astragalus membranaceus

Common Names:Huang qi, yellow leader, milk vetch

Family:Fabaceae

Part Used:Roots, rhizomes

Habitat:Astragalus is native to Mongolia and China. Cultivated in the U.S. and Canada

Astragalus is one of the most popular herbs in the traditional Chinese medicine system. It has been in use for over 2000 years. This herb is most often used as a diuretic and for lowering high blood pressure. Many people use it to treat upper respiratory infections as well as the common cold, as it seems to increase the production of white blood cells. Traditionally, this astragalus has also been used to increase energy, strengthen the immune system, treat excessive sweating, ulcers and diarrhea.

Bacopa

Scientific Name: Bacopa Monnieri

Common Names:Brahmi, Thyme-leafed gratiola, Coastal Waterhyssop, Water hyssop

Family:Scrophulariaceae

Part Used:Whole plant.

Habitat:Bacopa is native to India

Bacopa has been used as an effective brain tonic in the Ayurvedic system of medicine for thousands of years in India. It is beneficial to long and short term memory. The plant's saponins and bacosides have a positive effect on the brain's neurotransmitters and can help one to think faster. Bacopa is now being studied as a possible treatment for ADHD, Alzheimer's and Parkinson's disease. Bacopa is often used to treat depression, anxiety asthma, allergies and bronchitis. It also possess some anti-inflammatory properties.

Bearberry

Scientific Name: Arctostaphylos uva-ursi

Common Names:Uva ursi, mountain box, bear's grape, kinnikinnick

Family:Ericaceae

Part Used:Leaves

Habitat:Bearberry grows throughout the Northern Hemisphere

Bearberry is often taken as a tea. This herb is commonly used to treat urinary tract infections and inflammation of the urinary tract. It has astringent, diuretic and antiseptic properties.

CAUTION: This Bearberry can be toxic in high doses. Never take it if you are pregnant or if you have kidney disease. Do not give Bearberry to children.

Bee Balm

Scientific Name: Monarda didyma

Common Names:Wswego tea, mountain mint, scarlet bergamot

Family:Lamiaceae

Part Used:Leaves

Habitat:Bee Balm is native to North America

Bee Balm was often used by the Native Americans to treat intestinal problems, colic and flatulence. Tea made from this plant was used to induce sweating and break fevers. Bee balm is often used to treat the common cold and sore throat as well. The leaves of this plant are a good source of essential oil that contains thymol. Thymol is an antibiotic and often used as an ingredient in mouthwash.

Bee Pollen

Scientific Name: Entomophile pollen

Common Names:Honey bee pollen

Part Used:Pollen

Habitat:Bee pollen can be found on every continent except Antarctica

Though technically not a herb, bee pollen has been used by healers for thousands of years for it's health properties. It's rich in important vitamins, minerals, amino acids, enzymes, and trace minerals. It is a great source of easily digested and highly absorbable nutrition. Many people take it to increase energy.

CAUTION: Never consume bee pollen if you are allergic to bee stings.

Bilberry

Scientific Name: Vaccinium mytillus

Common Names:European blueberry, huckleberry, whortleberry

Family:Ericaceae

Part Used:Leaves, fruits

Habitat:Bilberry grows in the warm regions of the Northern Hemisphere

Bilberry has been used for centuries by European healers to treat such things as stomach cramps, diarrhea and diabetes. Now bilberry is most often used to prevent night blindness. It seems to be able to strengthen the capillaries and protect them from free radical damage. This plant contains flavonoids called anthocyanosides. These are a powerful antioxidant. In the past, bilberry has also been used as a remedy for varicose veins, hemorrhoids and bruising.

Black Cherry

Scientific Name: Prunus serotina

Common Names:Bird cherry, rum cherry

Family:Rosaceae

Part Used:Bark

Habitat:Black Cherry is native to North America

Native Americans used black cherry as a medicinal herb to treat coughs. The bark from the black cherry tree was often made into a tea or syrup and used to expel worms, heal ulcers and treat burns. They also used it as a remedy for sore throat, pneumonia and lack of appetite. Black Cherry bark contains a glycoside called prunasin. This substance quells spasms in the smooth muscles of the bronchioles, thus reducing the cough reflex.

Black Cohosh

Scientific Name: Cimicifuga racemosa

Common Names:Black snakeroot, macrotys, bugwort, bugbane

Family:Ranunculaceae

Part Used:Roots, rhizome

Habitat:Black Cohosh is native to North America

The Cherokee Indians used black cohosh as a diuretic and as a remedy for fatigue and tuberculosis. Other native Americans used this herb to treat menstrual irregularities, rheumatism and sore throat. Today, black cohosh is used mainly to reduce the severity of premenopausal and menopausal symptoms, such as excessive sweating, depression and hot flashes.

CAUTION: Black cohosh is not the same as blue cohosh. Blue cohosh may be toxic and has not been tested for safety.

Boneset

Scientific Name: Eupatorium perfoliatum

Common Names:Indian sage, feverwort, agueweed, sweat plant

Family:Compositae

Part Used:Leaves and flowers

Habitat:Boneset is native to North America

Boneset was used by the Native Americans to induce sweating and to treat colds, flu, arthritis, indigestion, loss of appetite, constipation, cholera, dengue, typhoid and malaria. This plant is still in use today to treat colds, flu, fever and minor inflammation.

CAUTION: Boneset may cause nausea, vomiting and diarrhea if consumed in large amounts. NEVER consume fresh boneset. It is toxic. It must be dried before consuming. Do not use it if you are pregnant or breast-feeding. People who are allergic to ragweed should not consume boneset.

Borage

Scientific Name: Borago officinalis

Common Names:Burrage, beebread, star flower, bee Plant, talewort

Family:Boraginaceae

Part Used:Flowers, seed oil

Habitat:Borage is native to Southern Europe

Borage is often used to treat fever, lung infections, inflammation of mucous membranes and as a diuretic. It may also be effective as a mild anti-depressant and sedative. Oil from Borage seeds are a rich source of gammalinolenic acid (GLA). GLA is a fatty acid used by the body to boost immunity and fight inflammation.

Boswellia

Scientific Name: Boswellia serrata

Common Names:Indian frankincense, Indian olibanum, dhup, and salai guggul

Family:Bruseraceae

Part Used:Resin

Habitat:Boswellia is native to Africa and Asia

Boswellia has been used in the Ayurvedic medicine system of India for over 2,000 years. Ancient healers used it to treat conditions such as asthma, fevers, cardiovascular disorders, rheumatism, and diabetes. Today, this herb is mostly used to treat inflammation and pain of the joints. The tree's resin contains boswellic acid that acts as a 5-LOX (5-lipoxygenase) inhibitor.

CAUTION: Boswellia may cause nausea and diarrhea, if taken in large quantities. Pregnant women should first talk to their doctor before taking this herb. It should not be taken by people with severe liver or kidney disease.

Buchu

Scientific Name: Agathosma betulina

Common Names:Buchu, boegoe, bucco, bookoo, diosma

Family:Rutaceae

Part Used:Leaves

Habitat:Buchu is native to South Africa

Buchu is most often used as a stimulating tonic and a diuretic. It is now commonly used to treat urinary tract infections. In the past, this herb has also been used to treat arthritis, kidney stones and gout. It can also be used externally for bruises and sprains.

Burdock

Scientific Name: Arctium Lappa

Common Names:Wild Burdock, gobo, burr, beggar's buttons

Family:Asteraceae

Part Used:Seeds, leaves and roots

Habitat:Burdock grows in the United States, Europe, Japan and China

Burdock was used by the ancient Greeks to treat wounds and infections. This herb is loaded with beneficial vitamins and minerals and is often used to treat liver and digestive problems, urinary tract infections, ulcers, eczema, psoriasis and to boost energy and stamina. It has anti-fungal and anti-bacterial properties and makes a good immune system booster and blood purifier.

Burdock is a strong detoxifier and could aggravate certain types of skin conditions before the healing process starts working. Burdock may interfere with several prescription drugs, like those for treating diabetes or blood sugar conditions. Pregnant or nursing women should talk with their doctor before taking this herb.

Butterbur

Scientific Name: Petasites hybridus

Common Names:Common butterbur, coughwort, pestilence wort

Family:Asteraceae

Part Used:Leaves, rhizomes

Habitat:Butterbur is native to Asia and Europe

Butterbur has traditionally been used to treat coughs, urinary problems, fever and to expel intestinal parasites. Now this herb is mostly used as an anti-inflammatory agent and to treat migraine headaches. It is sometimes used to reduce smooth muscle spasms. Some studies have found butterbur effective in reducing bronchial spasms in people having bronchitis and asthma. Butterbur extract is often just as effective as prescription antihistamines for treating allergic rhinitis and hay fever.

Calendula

Scientific Name: Calendula officinalis

Common Names:Pot marigold, poet's mairgold, Cape Weed

Family:Asteraceae

Part Used:Flowers

Habitat:Calendula is native to the Mediterranean region

Historically, calendula was used to induce menstruation, break fevers, cure jaundice, treat open sores and for liver and stomach problems. It has antiseptic and anti-inflammatory properties and can be used externally for sunburn and eczema. Today this herb is most often used externally to treat slow healing wounds and to promote tissue repair.

CAUTION: Do not take Calendula internally if pregnant or nursing. Could cause miscarriage.

Cascara Sagrada

Scientific Name: Frangula purshiana

Common Names:Cascara buckthron, california buckthory, sacred bark

Family:Rhamnaceae

Part Used:Bark

Habitat:Cascara Sagrada is native to the Pacific Northwest in North America

Cascara Sagrada was used by Native Americans as a laxative and to treat constipation, colitis, upset stomach, jaundice and hemorrhoids. Today it is sometimes used as a laxative.

CAUTION: Cascara Sagrada is not recognized as safe by the FDA. Cascara Sagrada is often too strong of a laxative and can cause intense stomach discomfort. A more gentle laxative, such as Psyllium is usually recommended. Do not take if pregnant.

Catnip

Scientific Name: Nepeta cataria

Common Names:Catmint, catswort, catnep, catrup

Family:Lamiaceae

Part Used:Flowers, Leaves

Habitat:Catnip is native to Asia and Europe

Medieval herbalists often used catnip to treat coughs, scalp irritations, bruises, restlessness and gas. Modern herbalists use this herb primarily to treat upset stomach, colic, colds, fever, flu and diarrhea. It is sometimes used to treat inflammation, allergies and as a mild sedative.

CAUTION: Do not take Catnip if you are pregnant or nursing. Catnip may stimulate the uterus and cause miscarriage. Do not give to children. Unsafe to smoke.

Cat's Claw

Scientific Name: Uncaria tomentosa
Common Names:Peruvian cat's claw, hawk's claw
Family:Rubiaceae
Part Used:Bark, root
Habitat:Cat's Claw is native to South and Central America

Cat's claw has been used by the natives of Peru for centuries to treat conditions such as asthma, bone pain, arthritis, urinary tract infections, ulcers and intestinal problems. Today, this herb is most often used to boost the immune system and as an anti-inflammatory. It is often taken for rheumatism and even to treat HIV and cancer.

CAUTION: Do not take Cat's Claw if pregnant or nursing. Do not give to children.

Cayenne

Scientific Name: Capsicum annuum

Common Names: Red pepper, capsicum, chili pepper

Family: Solanaceae

Part Used: Fruit

Habitat: Cayenne is native to tropical regions of the Americas

Cayenne was used by Native Americans as a pain reliever and to halt infections. It was also used for toothache, arthritis and to aid digestion. This herb has antibacterial properties, can stimulate blood flow and is rich in vitamins, minerals and antioxidants. Many people consume cayenne to maintain cardiovascular health. Studies suggest that it may be able to reduce triglyceride levels and platelet aggregation in the blood.

CAUTION: Hot peppers like Cayenne may irritate the skin. Use care when handling. Taking large amounts of Cayenne could cause stomach discomfort.

Chamomile

Scientific Name: Matricaria recutita

Common Names:German chamomile, wild chamomile

Family:Asteraceae

Part Used:Flower heads, oil

Habitat:Chamomile is native to Asia, Africa and Europe

Used by the ancient Egyptians for fever and chills, chamomile is still in wide use today. This plant is used for colic, indigestion, flatulence, bloating heartburn and to calm nervousness. Chamomile has anti-inflammatory, antifungal, antiseptic, antibacterial and antispasmodic properties. Some people suffering from peptic ulcers find relief from drinking chamomile tea.

CAUTION: Chamomile may cause allergic reactions in people sensitive to ragweed or other plants in the daisy family.

Chaparral

Scientific Name: Larrea tridentata
Common Names:Creosote bush, stinkweed, gobernadora, hediondilla
Family:Zygophyllaceae
Part Used:Leaves, twigs
Habitat:Chaparral is native to the U.S. and Mexico

Native Americans used chaparral for rheumatism, intestinal problems, colds, flu, bronchitis, diarrhea and urinary tract problems. They also chewed the twigs of this plant to relieve toothaches. Today chaparral is known to contain a powerful antioxidant and is being studied as a possible treatment for cancer.

Chaste Tree

Scientific Name: Vitex agnus-castus

Common Names:Chaste berry, vitex, agnus castus, monk's pepper, Abraham's balm

Family:Verbenaceae

Part Used:Fruits

Habitat:The chaste tree is native to Southern Europe and Western Asia

For over 2,500 years the chaste tree has been used to treat gynecological problems such as relieving menstrual cramps, promoting normal menstruation and to treat a host of other menstrual disorders. Today it still used for these same conditions. It is most commonly used to treat the symptoms of PMS.

CAUTION:NEVER take chaste tree if you are pregnant. Should not be taken with any type of hormone therapy.

Chicory

Scientific Name: Cichorium intybus

Common Names:Succory, wild succory, coffeeweed

Family:Asteraceae

Part Used:Whole herb

Habitat:Chicory is native to Asia, Europe and North America

Chicory was often used by the Native Americans for cleaning the blood, as a nerve tonic and diuretic. Today it is commonly used to treat loss of appetite and indigestion.

CAUTION: People with gallstones should not consume chicory.

Cinnamon

Scientific Name: Cinnamonum verum

Common Names:Chinese cassia, ceylon cinnamon, saigon cinnamon

Family:Lauraceae

Part Used:Bark

Habitat:Cinnamon is native to India. Cultivated in Indonesia, Africa and South America.

Cinnamon is most often used to soothe digestion, treat colds, nausea and inflammation. Cinnamon's essential oil has antifungal, antibacterial and antispasmodic properties.

Clubmoss

Scientific Name: Lycopodium clavatum

Common Names:Ground pine, stag's horn moss, wolf's claw moss, running pine

Family:Lycopodiaceae

Part Used:Whole plant

Habitat:Clubmoss is native to the Northern and Southern Hemispheres

Clubmoss has been used by ancient healers for over two thousand years. The druids used this plant as a laxative and purgative. Native Americans used it to treat postpartum pain, fever, weakness and to stop the bleeding of wounds. Today, clubmoss is used for kidney and urinary disorders, stomach upset, diarrhea and for treating skin conditions. This plant contains a substance called Huperzine which may be effective for memory problems and Alzheimer's disease. More studies on clubmoss have to be done to determine it's safety and effectiveness in this area.

Comfrey

Scientific Name: Symphytum officinale

Common Names:Knitbone, slippery root, blackwort

Family:Boraginaceae

Part Used:Leaves, roots

Habitat:Comfrey is native to Europe and Asia

Comfrey was used as a poultice by the ancient Greeks to stop bleeding. They also drank it as a tea for diarrhea and bronchitis.

CAUTION: Never take comfrey internally. Even though it was recommended by ancient healers in the past it has recently been shown to cause severe liver damage.

Cordyceps

Scientific Name: Cordyceps sinensis
Common Names:Caterpillar fungus, Zhiling, Cs-4
Family:Clavicipitaceae
Part Used:Fruiting body
Habitat:Cordyceps mushrooms grows wild on the Himalayan Plateau

This mushroom has a long history of use in Chinese herbalism. It is considered a great tonic for building physical strength and endurance. There is a substance in cordyceps which dilates the lung's airways, providing more oxygen to the blood. For this fact it is very popular with athletes. This healing mushroom is also used to treat asthma, cough and bronchitis. It possesses anti-inflammatory properties and has the ability to relax the bronchial walls. It's a great immune system booster as well.

Dandelion

Scientific Name: Taraxacum officinale

Common Names:Lion's tooth, blowball, fairy clock, wetweed, priests Crown

Family:Asteraceae

Part Used:Leaves, flowers, root

Habitat:Dandelion is native to Europe and Asia but grow all over the world

The dandelion was in use as far back as ancient China for it's medicinal properties. It was used as a potent diuretic and detoxifying herb. Other common uses of this plant were to treat breast inflammation, digestive disorders, appendicitis and to stimulate milk flow. European herbalists used dandelion as a remedy for eye problems, diarrhea, diabetes and fever.

Dong Quai

Scientific Name: Angelica sinensis

Common Names:Dang gui, tang-kuei, danggui, Chinese angelica

Family:Apiaceae

Part Used:Root

Habitat:This herb is native to China, Japan, and Korea

Often called female ginseng in China, Dong Quai is very popular with women there. It is used as a remedy for menstrual cycle disorder and to treat symptoms such as bleeding of the uterus and menstruation pain. It is helpful for relieving vaginal dryness, hot flashes, mood swings and PMS.

CAUTION: Never take Dong Quai if pregnant. Taking this herb could stimulate contractions of the uterus, which could lead to miscarriage.

Echinacea

Scientific Name: Echinacea purpurea

Common Names:Purple coneflower, coneflower, purple encinacea

Family:Asteraceae

Part Used:Roots, leaves and flowers

Habitat:Echinacea is native to Central and Eastern North America

Echinacea is very popular for treating colds and flu. This herb is a great immune system booster. Many people enjoy it as a healthy tea. Some of it's other uses are for treating sore throat and upper respiratory tract infections. It is a good detoxifier and has antiviral, anti-inflammatory and antibiotic properties.

Fo-Ti

Scientific Name: Polygonum Multiflorum

Common Names:He Shou Wu, climbing knotweed, flowery knotweed, Chinese cornbind, polygonum flower

Family:Polygonaceae

Part Used:Root

Habitat:Fo-Ti is native to China

Fo-Ti is a famous longevity herb that has been in constant use in China for thousands of years. It is very popular with older men and is said to be able to turn one's hair back to it's youthful color and appearance. This herb is also used to strengthen the lower back and knees. It can be used to strengthen the bones, tendons and muscles as well as to nourish blood.

CAUTION: Fo-Ti could cause stomach upset and diarrhea if taken in very large amounts.

Ginkgo Biloba

Scientific Name: Ginkgo biloba

Common Names:Ginkgo, bao gou, Yin-hsing, Maidenhair tree

Family:Ginkgoaceae

Part Used:Leaves and seeds

Habitat:Ginkgo biloba is native China but is also cultivated in Japan, France and the southern United States.

Ginkgo Biloba improves the flow of blood to the brain and increases oxygen to the brain cells. It is often used as an effective cognitive enhancer and memory booster.

Ginkgo possesses anti-coagulating properties and prevents the formation of blood clots. This could in turn reduce risk of stroke. This herb contains powerful antioxidants. Its terpenoids and flavonoids protect the body from free radical damage and cell oxidation.

CAUTION: Ginkgo can sometimes cause headaches and dizziness if taken in large doses. You should not take ginkgo if you are taking anti-depressants such as MAOI or SRRI medicines.

Gotu Kola

Scientific Name: Centella asictica

Common Names:Centella, Indian pennywort, Brahmi, Luei gong gen

Family:Mackinlayaceae

Part Used:Leaves, Stems

Habitat:Gotu Kola grows in Africa, North and South America, Asia, Australia and Madagascar

Gotu Kola has been used historically to relieve congestion from upper respiratory infections and colds and for wound healing. It is very popular for treating varicose veins and memory loss.

CAUTION: Gotu Kola should NEVER be taken by women who are trying to get pregnant. It should not be taken by pregnant or nursing women or children without talking to your doctor first. May cause sensitivity to sunlight and should never be taken by people with skin cancer.

Gynostemma

Scientific Name: Gynostemma Pentaphyllum
Common Names:Jiaogulan, southern ginseng, miracle herb, longevity herb, miracle tea, Jiao Gu Lan
Family:Cucurbitaceae
Part Used:Leaves
Habitat:Gynostemma is native to Japan, China, Korea, Vietnam

Gynostemma (Jiaogulan) is an adaptogen. It can bring your body into a state of balance. This herb is great for increasing strength and protecting the body and mind against stress. Gynostemma can boost the functioning of the immune system and is good for the digestive and cardiovascular systems.

CAUTION: Gynostemma should not be taken with herbs or medicines that affect immune system suppression or blood clotting.

Holy Basil

Scientific Name: Ocimum Sanctum

Common Names:Tulsi, Sacred basil, Surasa, Tulasi, Kemangen

Family:Lamiaceae

Part Used:Leaves, Stems

Habitat:Holy Basil is native to India

Holy Basil is used for reducing stress, anxiety and depression. It promotes health and wellbeing and protects the body and mind in a very positive way. It is also known to enhance cerebral circulation and improve memory.

CAUTION: Holy Basil has the ability to thin the blood and should not be taken along with blood thinning medications. It should not be taken by persons with hypoglycemia. It may decrease fertility and should never be taken by women trying to get pregnant. Never take if pregnant or nursing without first consulting your doctor.

Kava

Scientific Name: Piper Methysticum
Common Names:Kava, awa, ava pepper
Family:Piperaceae
Part Used:Rhizome, roots
Habitat:Kava grows on the Pacific Islands

Kava has been used by the people of the Pacific islands for hundreds of years as a natural anti-anxiety treatment. It has a very calming effect and puts most people in a good mood. It has also been used as a diuretic and to treat urinary problems, arthritis, asthma and upset stomach. It is very popular in Germany and often prescribed as the first line of treatment for anxiety disorders.

CAUTION: Some studies suggest that Kava could harm the liver. Never take this herb if you are pregnant or nursing. Could cause dry mouth and dizziness it taken in high doses.

Korean Ginseng

Scientific Name: Panax ginseng

Common Names:Korean ginseng, Asian ginseng, Oriental ginseng, Man root, root of immortality, Asiatic ginger

Family:Araliaceae

Part Used:Root

Habitat:Korean ginseng is native to Korea and China

Korean ginseng is an adaptogen. An adaptogen can help your body and mind handle stress better. This is an energizing herb often taken by people to ward off fatigue, increase strength, stamina and sharpen mental abilities. This herb is believed to lower cholesterol and may be helpful in treating diabetes and depression. Korean ginseng is a good immune system booster. Since it has a warming effect on the body, it's best taken in the winter months.

CAUTION: Taking large doses or prolonged use may not be good for people having high blood pressure. Taking high doses of this type of ginseng may cause irritability.

Lemongrass

Scientific Name: Cymbopogon citratus

Common Names:Silky heads, fever grass, barbed wire grass, tanglad, hierba Luisa, citronella grass or gavati chaha

Family:Poaceae

Part Used:Grass

Habitat:Lemongrass is native to tropical Asia and India

Lemongrass is used to treat many health conditions, such as cancer, stomach problems, nervous disorders, fevers, arthritis, flu, gas, pain and others. Lemongrass tea is a relaxing beverage that helps reduce anxiety and promotes sound sleep. Used externally, it can treat skin problems and keep the skin moist and clear.

CAUTION: Lemongrass should NOT be taken if pregnant since it has uterine stimulating properties.

Licorice Root, Chinese

Scientific Name: Glycyrrhiza Uralensis

Common Names:Guo Lao, sweat herb, sweet wood, beauty grass, elf grass, pink grass

Family:Legume

Part Used:Root

Habitat:Chinese licorice root is native to Asia

Chinese licorice root is very popular in the Chinese medicine system. It is added to many herbal formulas to enhance their effectiveness. Licorice is great to detoxify the body. It is able to remove over 1,200 toxins.

CAUTION: Do not take Chinese Licorice root if you suffer from heart disease or high blood pressure. Do NOT take if Pregnant or nursing. May cause the retention of water.

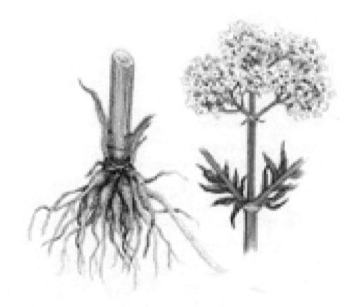

Lion's Mane

Scientific Name: Hericium erinaceus

Common Names:Satyr's beard, Hedgehog mushroom, Bearded hedgehog, Bearded tooth, Old man's beard, Sheep's head, Bear's head, Monkey's Head, Hedgehog, Pom Pom and Japanese yamabushitake

Family:Hericiaceae

Part Used:Fruiting Body

Habitat:The Lion's mane mushroom grows in Europe, Asia, and parts of North America

The Lion's mane mushroom is used to boost the immune system, promote digestive and colon health, improve the memory and relieve depression and anxiety. It is also used to lower blood pressure and stimulate the synthesis of Nerve Growth Factor. It is being considered as a treatment for dementia and Alzheimer's disease.

Lycium Fruit

Scientific Name: Lycium barbarum

Common Names:Goji, Chinese wolfberry

Family:Solanaceae

Part Used:Fruit

Habitat:Lycium grows in Northwestern China and Tibet

Lycium fruit has been consumed for centuries in China for its sweet taste and health giving properties. The berries from the Lycium plant are one of the most nutritious foods on earth. Besides supplying many vitamins and minerals to the body, these berries are often eaten for their high antioxidant value. Eating Lycium berries every day is believed to keep a person healthy well into old age.

CAUTION: Do not take if you have low blood pressure. Lycium can affect how quickly the liver breaks down some medications.

Maca

Scientific Name: Lepidium meyenii
Common Names:Peruvian ginseng
Family:Brassicaceae
Part Used:Root
Habitat:Maca is native to Peru

Maca is an adaptogen and helps the body cope with stress. This root is rich in vitamins, minerals, good fats, plant sterols and amino acids. Some people refer to it as a "superfood". The people of Peru found that consuming maca root could greatly enhance physical strength and stamina as well as boost the libido. It's a great overall energy booster and is popular with athletes. Maca is beneficial to the nervous system and is calming to the nerves. Today, this herb is mostly used for increasing energy and balancing the hormones.

CAUTION: Maca has a high iodine content and should not be consumed by people having thyroid disease. It has stimulant properties and could possibly raise the heart rate. It may not be safe for pregnant women to use maca supplements.

Milk Thistle

Scientific Name: Silybum marianum

Common Names:Silymarin, Marian Thistle, Mediterranean Thistle, Mary Thistle

Family:Asteraceae

Part Used:Seeds

Habitat:Milk Thistle is native to Europe

Milk thistle is a great protector of the liver and gallbladder. It can detoxify the blood and is often taken to treat cancer.

*Note Milk thistle was used in a few cases in Germany taken only 500 mg per day over a 6 month period cured liver cancer!

Maitake

Scientific Name: Grifola frondosa

Common Names:King of Mushrooms, Cloud Mushroom, Dancing Mushroom, Grifola, Hen of the Woods, Shelf Fungi

Family:Meripilaceae

Part Used:Root

Habitat:Maitake is native to China and Japan

The Maitake mushroom contains high amounts of vitamins, minerals and antioxidants. It is thought to be helpful in treating cancer and autoimmune disorders.

Rhodiola

Scientific Name: Rhodiola Rosea

Common Names:Golden Root, Arctic Root, Arctic Rose, Roseroot, Aaron's Rod

Family:Crassulaceae

Part Used:Root

Habitat:Rhodiola is native Siberia

Rhodiola rosea is very popular with Russian astronauts and athletes due to its ability to enhance physical strength and endurance. Also, taking rhodiola will allow the body to use less oxygen on a cellular level. Besides its beneficial effects on the body, this herb is often used to keep the mind sharp and improve memory. It is now gaining popularity as a natural anti-depressant. Rhodiola is considered an adaptogen. This means that it helps protect the body from all types of stress.

Saw Palmetto

Scientific Name: Serenoa repens

Common Names:Sabal palm, palmetto berry, sabal fructus, cabbage palm, American dwarf palm tree

Family:Palmae

Part Used:Fruit

Habitat:Saw Palmetto grows in the islands of the West Indies and Southeastern United States

Saw palmetto is a very popular herb with men over 40. It is often used to treat Benign Prostatic Hyperplasia (BPH) and it's symptoms, like painful urination and the need to urinate frequently. Another popular use of this herb is to treat male pattern baldness by reducing the body's levels of dihydrotestosterone (DHT). Too much DHT is believed to be what causes hair loss.

CAUTION: Do not take Saw palmetto if you take any blood thinning medication or if you have hemophilia, ulcers, or if you are planning any type of surgery. Taking this herb may increase the risk of bleeding.

Schizandra

Scientific Name: Schizandra chinensis

Common Names:Schisandra, Five flavor berry, Omicha, Wu wei zi, Magnolia vine

Family:Schisandraceae

Part Used:Fruit

Habitat:Schizandra is native to northern China

Schizandra berries are an adaptogen. Eating them may help you adapt to mental and physical stress more easily. It is packed with nutrition and gives one more energy. It is very beneficial to the skin.

CAUTION: Schizandra should not be taken by people who have gastroesophageal reflux disease (GERD), epilepsy, peptic ulcers or high brain (intracranial) pressure.

Shilajit

Scientific Name: Asphaltum

Common Names:Mineral Pitch, Vegetable Asphalt

Part Used:The resin

Habitat:Shilajit can be found in the Himalayan area, Nepal and Tibet.

Shilajit contains many vitamins and minerals and is often taken to increase longevity.

CAUTION: Do not take Shilajit if you suffer from gout. It can increase uric acid in the body. Children, pregnant or nursing mothers should always seek the advice of their doctor before taking.

Siberian Ginseng

Scientific Name: Eleutherococcus senticosus
Common Names:Siberian ginseng, eleuthero
Family:Araliaceae
Part Used:Root
Habitat:Siberian Ginseng is native to Russia, China and Korea

Siberian ginseng (Eleuthero) is considered an energizer and stress reducer. It has been used for hundreds of years as a invigorating tonic herb. It is a powerful adaptogen that can normalize the body and bring it back into balance.

It has been very popular with the Russian athletes and cosmonauts for its ability to protect the body and mind from stress and increase the capacity for hard mental and physical work. Many students take this type of ginseng for its beneficial effects. It is believed to help a person think more clearly and remember facts more easily.

CAUTION: If you have high blood pressure, talk to your doctor before taking Siberian ginseng.

Skullcap

Scientific Name: Scutellaria lateriflora

Common Names:Mad dog, Quaker bonnet, hoodwort, helmet flower, blue pimpernel

Family:Lamiaceae

Part Used:The whole plant

Habitat:Skullcap grows in Europe, Asia, Canada and the United States

Skullcap is an ancient sleep aid remedy. It can greatly reduce anxiety and nervousness. It is often called nature's tranquilizer. Besides its use as a sleep aid, many people take it to relieve muscle spasms and twitches, lower blood pressure and cholesterol. This herb also possesses anti-inflammatory properties and may be useful for treating arthritis and joint pain.

CAUTION:DO NOT TAKE while pregnant. Skullcap could cause miscarriage! Large doses of this herb may be harmful and could cause liver damage.

St. John's Wort

Scientific Name: Hypericum perforatum

Common Names:Johnswort, goat weed, hard hay, amber, klamath weed

Family:Hypericaceae

Part Used:

Habitat:St. John's Wort grows in Europe, The United States and Australia

St. John's Wort is known as Nature's anti-depressant. It is often used to treat depression and anxiety. It functions as an SSRI (selective serotonin reuptake inhibitor). This allows more serotonin to stay where it's needed to keep you feeling less depressed and anxious. This herb is also used to help quit smoking. St. John's work possesses antiviral properties and can be used externally to treat wounds.

CAUTION: This herb can exacerbate sunburn in fair skinned people.

Suma

Scientific Name: Pfaffia paniculata

Common Names:Brazilian ginseng, Para Todo

Family:Amaranthaceae

Part Used:Root

Habitat:Suma root is native to Latin America, Ecuador, Brazil, Peru, Panama and Venezuela

Suma is often called Brazilian ginseng due to it's ability to increase strength and stamina. Like all adaptogens, suma is good for reducing the ill effects of stress. This herb balances the hormones and is commonly taken to strengthen the adrenal glands. Suma contains germanium and so can boost the immune system. It contains many vitamins and minerals and has anti-inflammatory properties as well.

CAUTION: Suma could cause nausea if taken in large amounts.

Turmeric

Scientific Name: Curcuma longa
Common Names:Indian saffron, Jiang huang, Haridra
Family:Zingiberaceae
Part Used:Root
Habitat:Turmeric is native to India

Turmeric contains a powerful antioxidant called curcumin and is a great natural liver detoxifier.

CAUTION: Do NOT take Turmeric if pregnant or nursing. May possibly stimulate the uterus or promote a menstrual period. Should not be taken by people taking blood thinning medicine, as it can slow blood clotting. Could cause upset stomach, heartburn or nausea if taken in large amounts.

- Note on turmeric. To increase its effectiveness use with black pepper will increase it's strength by 2,000%!!!

Valerian root

Scientific Name: Valerian officinalis
Common Names:St. George's Herb, Set Well, Vandal Root, Fragrant Valerian, English Valerian, Amantilla
Family:Valerianaceae
Part Used:Root
Habitat:Valerian is native to Western Europe, Asia and North America

Valerian is an ancient remedy for insomnia and a great stress buster. Many people find it an effective treatment for anxiety as well. The active components in this herb increase the production of gamma amino butyric acid (GABA). The brain needs GABA to get to sleep faster and relax.

CAUTION: Valerian root should not be taken while pregnant. Do not give to children.

Goji Berry & Li Qing Yuen History

Lycium (also called "Chinese wolf berry") has been considered a major anti-aging herb for over 2,500 hundred years. It was described as a superior herb in the Spirit Farmer's Herbal. Tao Hong Jing (456-536 AD), a Taoist master and physician, wrote in his famous herbal classic "Commentary on the Spirit Farmer's Herbal," that "Lycium tonifies Jing and ch'i and strengthens the Yin Tao within a human."

There is an incredible Chinese story in which Lycium plays a major role. The very widespread knowledge of this story in Asia has made Lycium even more popular in China in the past century. One man, Li Qing Yuen, is said to have lived to be 252 years old. His life span has been verified by modern scholars. Born in 1678 in the mountainous southwest of China, he ran away from home at the age of eleven with three travelers. These travelers were in the herbal trade.

Together the boy and his three teachers traveled throughout China, Tibet, and Southeast Asia, encountering many dangerous situations, but all the while studying the herbal traditions of all the various regions.

As Li Qing Yuen became older, he became a practicing herbalist, and was well known for his amazing vigor and excellent health. Then one day, when he was around fifty years old, while out on a hike, he met a very old man who, in spite of his venerable old age, could out-walk Li Qing Yuen. This impressed Master Li very much because he believed that brisk walking was both a way to health and longevity and a sign of inner health. Li Qing Yuen inquired as to the old sage's secret. He was told that if every day he consumed a "soup" of Lycium he would soon attain a new standard of health. Li Qing Yuen did just that and continued to consume the soup daily until he was over one hundred and thirty years old !

Naturally, he was greatly revered by all those who knew him and he had many disciples who followed him. Even at this very old age, his sight was keen and his legs were strong, and he continued to take his daily vigorous walks. One day, he was on a journey through treacherous mountains. In the mountains he met a Taoist hermit who claimed to be five hundred years old. Humbled by the great illumination of the old Taoist, Li Qing Yuen begged the Taoist sage to tell him his secrets. The old Taoist, recognizing the sincerity of Li, taught him the secrets of Taoist Yoga (also known as Nei Gong, "the Inner Alchemy") and recommended that Li consume a daily dose of Panax Ginseng combined with Polygonum (Radix Polygonum multiflorum). Ginseng is well-known in the West; Polygonum multiflorum is not yet well-known here, but is highly prized in the Orient as a longevity herb, in the same class with ginseng. He continued to consume his Lycium soup daily.

It is said that Master Li also changed his diet so as to consume little meat or root vegetables and limited his consumption of grain. Instead, he lived mainly on steamed above-ground vegetables and herbs. He lived to be 252 years old, dying in 1930, reportedly after a banquet presented in his honor by a government official.

He had married during his lifetime fourteen times and lived through eleven generations of his own descendants, of which he had almost two hundred during two and a half centuries of life.

Though Li Qing Yuen's case is rare, in that it has been reasonably authenticated by both Eastern and Western scholars, tradition is rich in the Orient in the lore of Taoists living to ages unimaginable by us. It is well known that among the Chinese population, the Taoists far outlived all other people. Many lived to be centurions and few died prematurely. The Taoist art of longevity, known as the "Art of Radiant Health" is one of the great legacies of the East.

The herb Lycium has played a major part in Taoist health practice since ancient times. Though it is a common herb, it is one that the Taoists consider to be transcendental.

Latest scientific proof

Among geroprotectors, one of the most interesting compounds is derived from the traditional Chinese herbal medicine Huang Qi, Astragalus membrenaceus. **Astragalus** is traditionally used to "tonify ch'i," the intrinsic energy of the body. It's reported to lessen fatigue, boost immunity, and normalize blood pressure.

These effects have been well-studied by scientists who agree that astragalus improves physiological functions of the body that help us adapt better to the environment and resist disease. It may also slow the aging process by twenty-five percent!

This combined with regular exercise, fresh air, water, and periodic fasting could give an individual an extra 25-50 years of active life.

Chinese researchers found that two ingredients in **astragalus** may hold the key. Scientists believe that Astragaloside IV and Cycloastragenol work by activating an enzyme, telomerase, that protects telomere length—the bioactive tips of chromosomes that have a protective effect on our DNA.

One company in New York, T.A. Sciences, holds the patent on a natural, plant-based compound call TA-65 that is reported to rebuild telomere length. A generic version, Astragaloside IV, is available on the Internet. No one knows which of the two works best, or at all.

However, people will find out. With the availability of new, accurate telomere laboratory testing from Life Length and Telomere Diagnostics, you can measure your telomeres and track the progress of the effects of diet, lifestyle, and the benefits of geroprotectors.

This is one of the first times in history that non-scientists are taking medicines and testing a specific marker, telomere length, as well as recording their personal progress to see if they actually life healthier and longer.

The data for life long experiences taking astragalus will not be confirmed. However, nothing is stopping you from taking the herb now and surely it will do you no harm.

The three treasure's

In long-established Chinese traditions, the "Three Treasures" are the essential energies sustaining human life:

- **Jing** "nutritive essence, essence; refined, perfected; extract; spirit, demon; sperm, seed"
- **Ch'i** "vitality, energy, force; air, vapor; breath; spirit, vigor; attitude"
- **Shen** "spirit; soul, mind; god, deity; supernatural being"

This jing-qi-shen ordering is more commonly used than the variants qi-jing-shen and shen-qi-jing.

In internal alchemy practice, transmuting the Three Treasures is expressed through the phrases lianjing huaqi 鍊精化氣 "refining essence into breath", lianqi huashen 鍊氣化神 "refining breath into spirit", and lianshen huanxu 鍊神還虛 "refining spirit and reverting to Emptiness".

Both *Neidan* and Neo-Confucianism distinguish the three between xiantian 先天 "prior to heaven" and houtian 後天 "posterior to heaven", referring to Yuanjing 元精 "Original Essence", Yuanqi 元氣 "Original Breath", and yuanshen 元神 "Original Spirit".

The (2nd century BCE) Huainanzi refers to ch'i and shen with xing 形 "form; shape; body".

The bodily form (*xing*) is the residence of life; the ch'i fills this life while *shen* controls it. If either of them loses their proper position, they will all come to harm.

The Taoist text Gaoshang yuhuang xinyin jing (高上玉皇心印經, "Mind-Seal Scripture of the Exalted Jade Sovereign", or Xinyin jing "Mind-Seal Scripture") is a valuable early source about the Three Treasures.

Dating from the Southern Song dynasty (1127-1279), this anonymous text presents a simple and concise discussion of internal alchemy (neidan 內丹). In particular, it emphasizes the so-called Three Treasures (sanbao 三寶), namely, vital essence (jing 精), subtle breath (ch'i 氣), and spirit (shen 神).

Taoist patriarch instructs Sun Wukong "Monkey" with a poem that begins:

Know well this secret formula wondrous and true: Spare and nurse the vital forces, this and nothing else. All power resides in the semen (jing), the breath (ch'i), and the spirit (shen); Guard these with care, securely, lest there be a leak. Lest there be a leak!

Jing, 'the giver of life,' is the first of the three treasures according to Taoist principles. Jing is also 'essence' and as such it is a very dense and energy packed life promoting substance.

We receive our Jing from our parents, each providing their energies in the form of egg and sperm. But, in addition, the energy and Jing of all our ancestors are part of the mix! Our Jing is unique to us as we are unique to the world.

1) Jing essence exists in a stage of pure potential and becoming. It is a stored energy that can transform at any moment into what the Chinese refer to as 'the ten thousand things' or what we call creation. Jing is not only used to create another human being, it can also be used to create thoughts, works of art, symphonies, novels, and companies. Anything that the mind can create is a manifestation of   Jing.

In the body, Jing is traditionally associated with the Kidneys, spinal fluid, brain, skeletal structure, and bone marrow. Jing Essence must be protected and nourished if we are to experience healthy aging and longevity.

Our life choices, what we choose to eat, how we choose to act, and how much rest we give ourselves all have a direct impact on the quality and quantity of our Jing essence.

Ch'i energy is depleted by living itself, but most especially by stress, excessive behavior, and overwork.

Jing can be re-acquired and replenished through the consumption of certain rare herbs(ginseng, Ho Shou Wu, Goto kola, etc.) which contain this treasure.

Jing herbs are divided into two categories: Yin and Yang tonics. Some Yin and Yang herbs can be used singularly because they are so well balanced. Sophisticated formulations have been developed over the centuries that build *Yin* and *Yang* energy and these are created by blending *Yin* herbs and *Yang* herbs. The secret of rejuvenation and in maintaining our health lies in rebuilding the right balance of *Yin* and *Yang*. These *Yin* and *Yang* tonic herbs tend to be mild and are very well tolerated in both the short and long term by most people. Everybody needs some *Yin* and *Yang* tonification, so finding an appropriate combination is very important.

Some *Yin* and *Yang* tonics are almost universally tolerated and may be used by anyone. *Yin* herbs are deeply nourishing. They replenish spent *Jing* and build reserves that are stored in the body for future use. They are famed for their long term regenerative qualities.

They are generally moistening and are believed to be youth preserving. *Yin* herbs should be consumed by people who have depleted their *Yin* reserves. Life itself depletes *Yin*, and *Yin* is constantly consumed as we grow older, until by middle age many people experience *Yin* depletion. Yin tonic herbs tend to nourish endocrine hormones, which are noticeably depleted as one grows older. Besides aging, *Yin* is also specifically depleted by stress, overwork, exhaustion, childbearing, excessive or chronic drug or medicine use, disease, excessive emotionalism and sexual excess.

Those who are deficient in **Yin Jing** tend to be chronically exhausted, and they tend to have dark rings under their eyes, backaches, weak kidney and reproductive functions, low resistance to infection, weak digestion and show signs of rapid aging, including dryness and wrinkling of the skin. Yin Jing herbs are capable of replenishing the treasure and building reserves for the future. Thus Yin Jing herbs are considered in Asia to be the cornerstone of rejuvenation and the foundation of longevity.

Yang herbs are deeply empowering. The rekindle the fire of life where it has been spent and invigorate vigor at the deepest levels. They are famed for their rejuvenative, deeply invigorating qualities. Yang herbs are used to build sexual energy, creative power, will power and athletic power. The result of consuming Yang Jing herbs is a renewed youthfulness. However, Yang energy tends to be warm and invigoration and therefore requires Yin to maintain coolness and balance. Yang herbs should be accompanied by Yin herbs. This is especially true for those who are suffering from Yin deficiency.

If you wish to utilize Yang herbs, build up the *Yin* Jing first until the signs of Yin deficiency are eliminated. This may take some time, but regular consumption of powerful Yin Jing herbs will surely nurture the deep Yin. Eventually Yang herbs can be consumed and that is when the healing begins.

Some people may experience hot symptoms and dryness, and still be Yang deficient. It is possible to be both *Yin* and *Yang* deficient but to be more *Yin* deficiency. This will result in what is known as "false fire," where the person will experience heat, inflammation, low grade fevers, hot flashes, etc. These people will certainly need to consume a lot of *Yin* Jing herbs, but they may also need to consume a small amount of *Yang* Jing herbs if they also lack any power.

Jing, or essence, is seen as the source of life and is the most dense of the three Treasures. According to tradition, Jing is received from the mother at conception and contains our heritage and directs the growth patterns (like the DNA).

It is said to be the material basis for the physical body and nourishes, fuels, and cools the body. This essence is a Yin characteristic and is the aspect of the body that is responsible for all development.

It is believed that the original essence received at conception can never be replaced if lost, but can be supplemented and acquired from the right food and herbs. Many of the best tonic herbs for healthy aging and retaining a youthful body support the essence. Proper lifestyle habits, such as sound sleep at night also help to preserve the essence.

Once you are born, original essence is the fountainhead and root of your life. It is what enables you to grow stronger and bigger. After your birth you start to absorb the essence of food and air, converting these essences into the ch'i (energy) which supplies your body's needs. It does not matter how much original essence you have carried over from your parents. If you know how to conserve it, you will have more than enough for your lifetime.

According to Chinese medicine, you probably cannot increase the amount of essence you have. It is believed, however, that ch'i-kung training can improve its quality.

In ch'i-kung training, knowing how to conserve and firm your original jing is of primary importance. To conserve means to refrain from abusing your original jing through overuse. For example, if you overindulge in sexual activity you will lose original jing faster than other people will and your body will degenerate faster (this is what I witness most men and women doing especially early in life). To firm your Jing means to keep and protect it. For example, you should know how to keep your kidneys strong. Kidneys are thought of as the residence of original jing. When your kidneys are strong, the original jing will be kept firm will not be lost. Therefore conserving and firming your essence is the first step in training. In order to know how to conserve and firm your essence, you must first know the root of this jing, where the original jing resides, and how original jing is converted into ch'i (energy).

The root of your original jing before your birth is in your parents. After birth that original jing stays in its residence, the kidneys which are now also its root. When you keep this root strong, you will have plenty of original jing to supply your body.

If you look carefully and how you were formed, you can gain interesting insights into life. You started as o-ne sperm which, because it managed to reach and penetrate the egg before any of the other millions of sperm could, was o-ne of the strongest and luckiest sperm alive. O-nce this sperm entered the egg, o-ne human cell formed and then started to divide, from o-ne into two, and from two into four. Then on and on into a fetus, then a baby. All of the baby's health depended o-n the sperm and egg, which are generated from the essence of the parents. As the baby was being formed it was immersed in liquid, and received all of its nutrition and oxygen from the mother through the umbilical cord.

Notice that the umbilical cord connects at the navel, which is very close to both the lower belly (solar plexus) and the body's center of gravity. The umbilical cord is very long, and because it is hard for the mother alone to push the necessary supplies to the baby, the baby needs to help. The baby must draw the nutrients to itself with an in and out pumping motion of its abdomen.

Once you are born, you start taking in oxygen through your nose and food through your mouth. Since you no longer need the abdominal motion to pump in nutrients, it gradually stops, and, finally, you forget how to use it. In ch'i-kung, the abdomen is still considered the original energy source because it is here that energy is made from the original jing, which you inherited from your parents. This original jing is converted continuously into energy, which moves into the lower abdomen, and stays stored there in its residence for future use. The lower belly is located on the Conception Vessel-one of the eight energy reservoirs in the body which regulate that energy flow in the other energy channels.

Lower belly energy is considered a Water Energy, and is able cool down the Fire Energy which is generated from the essence of food and air and which resides at the solar plexus.

As you may realize from the above discussion, if you wish to stay strong and healthy, you must first conserve your original Jing. Remember that Original Jing is like the principle in your savings account in that it is an original investment that will continue to return interest as long as it is conserved. Essence can produce energy, so if you handle this essence carefully, you will continue to have essence and energy. However, if you abuse yourself with an unhealthy lifestyle, you may damage and reduce your original essence.

In order to conserve your essence, you must first control your sexual activity. The gonads are called the external kidneys in Chinese medical society. This is because Chinese doctors believe that sperm is a product of original jing and the essence from food and air. **The more ejaculations you have, the faster you will exhaust your original jing and the shorter your life will be.**

It is important to understand that Chinese doctors and ch'i kung practitioners are not saying that in order to conserve your essence, you must stop your sexual activity completely. As a matter of fact, they encourage the proper amount of sexual activity, believing that it will energize and activate the essence, which makes the essence-energy conversion more efficient. Remember: essence is like fuel, and ch'i is like the energy generated from this fuel. The more efficiently you can convert your fuel into energy, though lest you waste.

In addition, the proper amount of sexual activity will revitalize the energy so that it nourishes the spirit. This will help you stay mentally balance, and raise your spirit. It's very important to keep your spirit raised, otherwise you will tend to get depressed and will be afraid to face life. It is very hard to define how much sex is the proper amount.

It depends in the individual's age and state of health. According to ch'i kung, the essence, which resides in the gonads is the main source of the energy, which fills up the four major energy vessels in the legs.

These four energy reservoirs keep the legs strong and healthy. Therefore, if you feel your legs are weak due to the amount of sexual activity, you have lost too much of your Jing.

The second thing you must do in order to conserve your original jing is to prevent your original jing from leaking out of your body. There are two acupuncture cavities called jing storage or jing doors. These two cavities are the doors through which your kidneys communicate with the outside, and are used to regulate the energy production in the kidneys. When energy is converted from original essence, most of it moves forward to the lower belly. However, some energy is lost backwards through the kidney doors. If you lose too much energy, your essence will be depleted as you try to make up for the loss. In ch'i kung practice, o-ne of the major training goals is to learn how to lead converted energy from the kidneys to the abdomen more efficiently.

2) Ch'i, 'the breath of life' is the second of the Three Treasures. This is what is referred to when most people speak about 'energy.' Everything in creation is composed of ch'i in one form or another. In the teachings of Classical Chinese Medicine, human beings are concerned with two major forms of ch'i, prenatal and postnatal. Pre-natal ch'i is the energy that is donated and supplied by a mother during the development of her child. After the mother gives birth, the child then becomes independent of the mother's energy system and will then begin to use its post-natal ch'i to support its life, growth, and development.

In Classical Chinese Medicine, ch'i has five major functions in the human body. The first is movement, that includes the movement and function of all organ systems in the body as well as the muscles. The second is warming, as in maintaining a constant body temperature. The third is protecting, this usually refers to the immune system and all of its functions. The fourth is holding, this has to do with holding all the organs and tissues in their proper place and also holding the blood in the vessels. The fifth is transformation, and this may be one of the most important because all human biological and physiological processes are based on the transformation of ch'i.

Lastly, the production of postnatal ch'i in the body is related to two major organ systems, the lungs and the digestive system (spleen and stomach). The reason we call ch'i the 'breath of life' is that is has such an intimate relationship with the Lungs. Through the transformation of the food we eat and the air we breathe, the body is able to digest and assimilate nutrients to sustain our lives.

The quality of our the air we breathe and the food that we choose to eat will have a direct impact on the quality and quantity of the ch'i we are able to produce on a minute to minute and day to day basis.

The second treasure is known as ch'i (pronounced *Chee*). ch'i is translated as vitality. ch'i is the energy of life that we acquire through breathing and eating and manifests as our day to day vitality. Ch'i tonics are also divided into two categories: Ch'i (energy) tonics and blood tonics. These ch'i and blood tonics are important in the maintenance of day to day health and vitality, our resistance to disease and our ability to cope with stress.

Ch'i tonics fortify the digestive, respiratory and immune functions and are necessary for true health. Ch'i tonics also help build muscle and develop muscular strength. blood tonics help build blood and nourish all the tissues of the body.

It is said that "men are governed by ch'i and women are governed by blood. This means that men generally benefit by consuming more ch'i tonics while women generally benefit by consuming more blood tonics. This does not mean that men do not need blood and women do not need ch'i. It is simply a matter of natural balance. Everybody should consume some amount of ch'i and blood tonics regularly according to need.

Most ch'i tonics are powerful adaptogens. That means they have significant double-direction activity as it relates to our stress responses, our immune functions and our metabolic functions. Every human can benefit from the consumption of adaptogenic herbs.

Ch'i gives us the ability to activate and move our bodies and is generally thought of as the vital force within all things living. Ch'i corresponds broadly to energy and matter, and every phenomenon in the Universe is a manifestation of ch'i. When Qi is condensed it can manifest as matter (it' s Yin form) and when it disperses it manifests as energy (Yang). ch'i travels through the 12 meridians (channels) of the body very much like blood through vessels, providing life and movement. Chinese medicine works to ensure that ch'i is able to move freely through these meridians, that it is moving in the correct direction, and that it is available in abundance. When it is, the body is balanced and healthy. An ancient quote dated from 200 BC describes it this way: *"A human being results from the ch'i of heaven and earth. The union of the ch'i of heaven and earth is called a human being"*. ch'i also protects the body against external and internal pathological factors, and is the source of production of blood, tears, sweat, and urine. ch'i also warms the body through the mechanism of energy transfer through movement.

Ch'i

Since we have already discussed ch'i (energy) in general terms, we will now discuss energy in the human body and in ch'i kung training. Before you start there is o-ne important thing you should know. At this time, there is no clear explanation of the relationship between all of the circulatory systems and the energy circulatory system. The Western world knows of the blood system, nervous system, and lymphatic system. Now, there is the energy circulation system from China. How are, for example, the energy and the nervous system related? If the nervous system does not match the energy system, where does the sensing energy in the nervous system

How is the lymphatic system related to the energy system? All of these questions are still waiting for study by modern scientific methods and technology. Here are o-nly some of the theoretical assumptions based o-n the research conducted up to now.

Chinese medical society believes that the energy and blood are closely related. Where energy goes, blood follows. It is believed that ch'i provides energy for the blood cells to keep them alive. As a matter of fact, it is believed that blood is able to store energy, and that it helps to transport Air Energy especially to every cell of your body.

If you look carefully, you can see that the elements of your physical body such as the organs, nerves, blood, and even every tiny cell are all like separate machines, each with their own unique function. Just like electric motors, if there is no current in them, they are dead. If you compare the routes of the blood circulatory system, the nervous system, and the lymphatic system with the course of the energy channels, you will see that there is a great deal of correspondence. This is simply because ch'i is the energy needed to keep them all alive and functioning.

Now look at your entire body. Your body is composed of two major parts. The first part is your physical body, and the second is the energy supply, which your body needs to function. Your body is like a factory. Inside your body are many organs, which correspond to the machines required to process the raw materials into the finished product. Some of the raw materials brought into a factory are used to create the energy with which other raw materials will be converted into finished goods. The raw materials for your body are food and air and the finished product is life.

The energy in your body is analogous to the electric current, which the factory power plant obtains from coal or oil. The factory has many wires connecting the power plant to the machines, and other wires connecting telephones, intercoms, and computers. There are also many conveyor belts, elevators, wagons, and trucks to move material from o-ne place to another. It is no different in your body, where there are systems of intestines, blood vessels, complex networks of nerves and energy channels to facilitate the supply of blood, sensory information and energy to the entire body. However, unlike the digestive, circulatory, and central nervous systems energy channels are non-material and cannot be observed as physical objects. The circulatory, nervous, and energy systems all posses similar configurations within the body, and are distributed rather equally throughout the body.

In a factory, different machines require different levels of current. It is the same for your organs, which require different levels of energy. If a machine is supplied with an improper level of power, it will not function normally and may even be damaged. In the same way, your organs, when the energy level running to them is either too positive or too negative, will be damaged and will degenerate more rapidly.

The ancient Chinese character for ch'i (energy) was formed of two words. o-n the top is the word "nothing" and at the bottom is the word "fire." This implies that Qi is "no fire." That means that when the organs are supplied with the proper amount of energy, they will not be overheated and "on fire."

In order for a factory to function smoothly and productively, it will not o-nly need high quality machines, but also a reliable power supply. The same goes for your body. The quality of your organs is largely dependent upon what you inherited from your parents. To maintain your organs in a healthy state and to insure they function well for a long time, you must have an appropriate energy supply. If you don't have it, you will become sick.

Ch'i (energy) is affected by the quality of air you inhale, the kind of food you eat, your lifestyle, and even your emotional make-up and personality. The food and air are like the fuel or power supply and their quality affects you. Your lifestyle is like the way you run the machine, and your personality is like the management of the factory. This metaphor is an oversimplification.

The behavior and function of ch'i (energy) is much more complex and difficult to handle than the power supply in a factory. You are neither a robot nor a factory; you are a human being with feelings and emotions. Unfortunately, your feelings have a major influence o-n your energy circulation. For example, when you pinch yourself, the energy in that area will be disturbed. This energy disturbance will be sensed through the nervous system and interpreted by your brain as pain. No machine can do this. Moreover, after you have felt the pain, unlike a machine, you will react either as a result of instinct or conscious thought. Human feelings and thought affect energy circulation in the body whereas a machine cannot influence its power supply. In order to understand your energy, you must use your feelings, rather than just the intellect, to sense its flow and make judgments about it.

Now a few words as to the source of human energy;

As mentioned, a lot of Chinese doctors, martial artists and ch'i kung practitioners believe that the body contains two general types of energy. The first type is called pre-birth energy or original energy. Original energy is also called pre-heaven energy. Here, heaven means the sky so pre-heaven means before the baby has seen the sky. In other words, before birth. Original Energy comes from converted original essence, which you received before your birth. This is why original energy is also called pre-birth energy.

The second type is called post birth energy which means post heaven energy. This energy is drawn from the essence of the food and air we take in. As mentioned, the residence of the post birth energy is in the solar plexus. This energy then circulates down and mixes with pre birth or lower body energy (original energy.) Together, they circulate down, passing into the governing vessel, from where they are distributed to the entire body.

Pre birth energy is commonly called water energy because it is able to cool down the post birth energy, which is called fire energy. Fire energy brings the body to a positive state, which stimulates the emotions and scatters and confuses the mind. When the water energy cools your body down, the mind will become clear, neutral and centered. It is believed in ch'i kung circles that fire energy supports the emotional part of the body, while water ch'i supports the wisdom part.

After the fire energy and water energy mix, this energy will not o-nly circulate to the governing vessel, but will also supply the thrusting vessel, which will lead the energy directly up through the spinal chord to nourish the brain and energize the spirit and soul. Energizing the brain and raising the spirit are very important in chi kung practice.

According to its function, energy can be divided into two major categories. The first is called Managing Energy, because it manages or controls the functioning of the body. This includes the functioning of the brain and the organs and even body movement. Managing Energy is again divided into two major types. The first type circulates in the channels and is responsible for the functioning of the organs. The circulation of energy to the organs and the extremities continues automatically as long as you have enough energy in your reservoirs and you maintain your body in good condition. The second type of Managing Energy is linked to your mind. When your mind decides to do something, for example, to lift a box, this type of mind energy will automatically flow to the muscles needed to do the job. This type of energy is directed by your thoughts, and therefore is related closely to your feelings and emotions.

The second major category of energy is guardian energy. Guardian energy forms a shield o-n the surface of the body to protect you from negative outside influences. Guardian energy is also involved in the growth of hair, the repair of skin injuries, and many other functions o-n the surface of the skin. Guardian energy comes from the energy channels and is led through the millions of tiny channels to the surface of the skin. This energy can even reach beyond the body. When your body is positive, this energy will be strong, and your pores will open. When your body is negative, this energy is weak, and your pores will close up more to prevent energy from being lost.

In the summertime, your body is positive and your energy is strong, so your energy shield will be bigger and will extend beyond your physical body, and the pores will be wide open. In the wintertime, your body is relatively negative, and you must conserve your energy in order to stay warm and keep pathogens out. The energy shield is smaller and does not extend out much beyond your skin.

Guardian energy functions automatically in response to changes in the environment, but it is also influenced significantly by your feelings and emotions. For example, when you feel happy or angry, the energy shield will be more open than when you are sad.

In order to keep your body healthy and functioning properly, you must keep the Managing Energy functioning smoothly and, at the same time, keep the guardian energy strong to protect you from negative outside influences such as the cold. Chinese doctors and ch'i kung practitioners believe that the key to doing this is through Shen (spirit.) Spirit is considered to be the headquarters, that directs and controls the energy. Therefore, when you practice ch'i kung, you must understand what your spirit is and know how to raise it. When people are ill and facing death, very often the ones with a strong spirit, which is indicative of a strong will to live, will survive. The people who are apathetic or depressed will generally not last long. A strong will to live raises the spirit, which energizes the body's ch'i (energy) and keeps you alive and healthy.

In order to raise your spirit, you must first nourish the brain with energy. You energize the brain so you can concentrate more effectively. Your mind will then be steady, your will strong, and your spirit raised.

Energy you take in from food and air warms the body. This is called Fire Energy and is associated with emotions. Water energy (or original energy) is generated from original Essence. It has its root in the kidneys, has a cooling effect o-n the body, and is associated with wisdom and the mind.

As a ch'i kung practitioner, in addition to paying attention to the food and air you take in, it is important that you learn how to generate water energy and how to use it more effectively. Water energy can cool down the fire energy and, therefore, slow down the degeneration of the body. Water energy also helps to calm your mind and keep it centered. This allows you to judge things objectively. During

Qigong practice, you will be able to sense your energy and direct it effectively.

In order to generate Water Energy and direct it efficiently, you must know how and where it is generated. Since water energy comes from the conversion of Original Essence, they both have the kidneys for their root. Once water energy is generated, it resides in the solar plexus below your navel. In order to conserve your water energy, you must keep your kidneys firm and strong.

3) Shen, 'the light of life' is the third of the Three Treasures. This is the most refined and immeasurable of the energies. It is translated as 'Spirit,' but it is much more than just our spirit. It is our consciousness. Our higher self. Our connection to the Divine. Shen is housed in the Heart, and when abundant, provides us with feelings of peace, calm, and serenity. It gives us proper perspective on our life and our place in the universe. Compassion and empathy for others are hallmarks of awakened Shen.

What is important to understand about Shen, is that it ultimately is best cultivated by mastering

Jing and Qi and the body. It is similar to a pregnancy, when the egg and sperm are united, a soul naturally attaches to the new life. When we are jing and ch'i deficient or out of balance, we do not have the vehicle best suited for housing the highest vibration of Shen energy. When jing and ch'i are properly balanced, nourished, and united, Shen can flourish! That is why it is so important to protect, nourish, and balance all Three Treasures.

The shen is revealed to others through the eyes. It is also visible in our face, our expressions, our smile, our alertness. When shen is strong, we have mental acuity and sharpness. Our imagination is activated. We become channels of energy. We are in the great immortal flow of life!

The third treasure is called shen. Shen is the energy of consciousness and awareness. Though there is no precise translation for shen, it is often translated as spirit. Shen is the vitality and stability of the mind and of the human spirit. A person with strong shen is one who is calm and at peace, strong minded, aware, clear, centered, deeply intelligent and profoundly happy.

A person who is kind, generous and giving and who has a big heart is said to have a lot of shen. Great shen manifests as great love. From a spiritual perspective, shen is the ultimate treasure.

Certain herbs have been found through the centuries to enhance this shen energy. Shen tonics generally have a mild calming quality. When combined into an herbal program that is taken daily, shen tonic formulation will have profound effects on our state of mind and body.

Tonic herbs can be categorized as jing (yin and/or yang), ch'i (energy and/or blood) and shen (opening and/or stabilizing) by virtue of which treasure(s) they tend to nourish and develop.

Shen, or Spirit, is the most subtle of the three Treasures and is the vitality behind jing and ch'i. The shen represents the forces that shape our personality including the mental and spiritual aspects. The heart houses the shen, and this can be seen in healthy individuals through a certain brightness of the eyes. Shen disturbances generally manifest as mental and emotional disorders. While the shen is often referred to as the spirit, it can be better understood as a person's inner light. Our Shen allows us to think and discriminate, and shapes our personality. Shen is the most immaterial of the three Treasures, hence it's association with the word "Spirit".

It is very difficult to find an English word to exactly express Shen.

When you are alive, shen is the spirit directed by the mind. When your mind and spirit are not steady they are not peaceful. The average person can use his emotional mind to energize and stimulate his spirit (shen) to a higher state, but at the same time he must restrain his emotional mind with his wisdom mind. If his mind can control his emotional mind (xin) then the mind, as a whole, will be concentrated and able to govern the spirit. When someone's spirit is excited, however, it is not being controlled by his mind thus his spirit, and his will, are not clear.In ch'i kung it is important to train your wisdom mind to control your emotional mind effectively. In order to reach this goal, Buddhists and Taoists train themselves to be free of emotions. Only in this way are they able to build a strong spirit that is completely under their control.

When you are healthy you are able to use your mind to protect your spirit at its residence: the forehead. Even when your spirit is energized, it is still controlled. However, when you are very sick or near death, your mind becomes weak and your spirit will leave its residence and wander around. When you die, your spirit separates completely from the physical body. It is then called a Soul.

The Chinese believe that when your spirit reaches a higher and stronger state, you are able to sense and feel more sharply, and your mind is more clever and inspired. The world of living human beings is usually considered a Negative World. It is believed that when your spirit reaches this higher, sensitive state you can transcend your mind's normal capacity. Ideas beyond your usual grasp can be understood and controlled, and you may develop the ability to sense or even communicate with the Positive World.

This supernatural spirit (Ling) is sharp, clever, nimble and able to quickly empathize with people and things. It is believed that when you die this supernatural spirit continues to hold your spirit in the positive world as a "spiritual ghost" temporarily.

It is believed that if this supernatural spiritual soul is strong enough, it will live for a long time after the physical body is dead and have plenty of opportunity to reincarnate. Chinese people believe that if a person has reached the stage of enlightenment or Buddhahood when he is alive, after he dies this supernatural spirit will leave the cycle of reincarnation and live forever, implying that they have reached the divine. Normally, if you die and your supernatural spiritual soul is not strong, your spirit has only a short time to search for a new residence in which to be reborn before its energy disperses. In this case, the spirit becomes a ghost.

Buddhists and Taoists believe that when you are alive you may use your essence and energy to nourish the spirit and make your soul strong. When this "soul spirit" is built up to a high level, your will is able to lead it to separate from the physical body even while you are alive. When you have reached this stage, your physical body is able to live for many hundreds of years. People who can do this are called many things including "immortal," "fairy," or "god." Throughout, this refers to a living person whose spirit has reached the stage of enlightenment or Buddhahood.

The foundation of Buddhist and Taoist ch'i kung training is to firm your spirit, nourish it, and grow it until it is mature enough to separate from your physical body. In order to do this, a ch'i kung practitioner must know where the spirit resides and know how to keep, protect, nourish, and train it. It is also essential for you to know the root or origin of your spirit.

Your spirit resides in the forehead, in the place often known as the third eye. When you concentrate o-n the forehead, the spirit can be formed (kept and protected.) When someone's mind is scattered and confused, his spirit is not at its residence and wanders.

According to ch'i kung theory, through your emotional mind is able to raise up your spirit, your mind can also make it confused so that it leaves its residence. You must use your mind constantly to restrain and control your spirit at its residence.

In ch'i kung, when your energy can reach and nourish your spirit efficiently, your spirit will be energized to a higher level and, in turn, conduct the energy in its circulation. Spirit is the force which keeps you alive, and it is also the control tower for the ch'i (energy). When your spirit is strong your energy is strong and you can lead it efficiently. When your spirit is weak, your energy is weak and the body will degenerate rapidly. Likewise, ch'i supports the spirit, energizing it and keeping it strong, sharp, and clear. If the energy in your body is weak, your spirit will also be weak.

Once you know the residence of your spirit, you must understand the root of your spirit, and learn how to nourish it and make it grow. We have already discussed original essence, which is the essential life you have inherited from your parents. After your birth, this original essence is your most important energy source. Your original energy is created from this original essence, and it mixes with the energy generated from the food you eat and the air you breathe to supply the energy for your growth and activity. Naturally, this mixed energy is nourishing your spirit as well. While the fire energy will strengthen your spirit, water energy will strengthen the mind to control the energized spirit. The spirit which is kept in its residence by the mind, which is nourished by the original energy is called original spirit (yuan shen.) Therefore, the root of your Original Spirit is traced back to your original essence. When your spirit is energized but restrained by your mind it is called essence spirit (jing shen, also "spirit of vitality.")

Original Spirit is thought of as the center of your being. It is able to make you calm, clear your mind, and firm your will. When you concentrate your mind o-n doing something, it is called "gathering your essence to meet your spirit." This implies that when you concentrate, you must use your original essence to meet and lift up your original spirit, so that your mind will be calm, steady, and concentrated.

Since this spirit is nourished by your original energy, which is considered water energy, original spirit is considered water spirit. For those who have reached a higher level of ch'i kung practice, cultivating the spirit becomes the most important subject.

For Buddhists and Taoists the final goal of cultivating the spirit is to form or generate a holy embryo from their spirit and nourish it until the spiritual baby is born and can be independent. For the average ch'i kung practitioner however, the final goal of cultivating spirit is to raise the spirit through energy nourishment while maintaining control with the mind. This raised spirit can direct and govern the energy efficiently to achieve health and longevity.

It is very important to point out that your spirit (shen) and your brain cannot be separated (while you are alive). Shen is the spiritual part of your being and is generated and controlled by your mind. The mind generates the will, which keeps your spirit firm. The Chinese commonly use spirit (Shen) and will (Zhi) together as "Shen Zhi" because they are so related. In addition you should understand that when your spirit is raised and firm, this raised spirit will firm your will. They are mutually related, and assist each other. From this you can see that the material foundation of the spirit is your brain. It is said "nourish your spirit" it means "nourish your brain." The original nourishing source is your original essence. This essence is then converted into energy, which is led to the brain to nourish and energize it. In ch'i kung practice, this process ("Fan Jing Bu Nao") means "return the essence to nourish the brain. This may be increased by doing reverse gravity type exercise, such as; handstands, hanging by your legs from a bar or tree limb, head or neck stands on the ground.

In Taoist literature, you will frequently read about both "Yi" (Intent) and "Xin" (Emotion) at different times to mean "mind," often confusing people who are not familiar with the Chinese language. Before advancing any further, you should first be sure that you have a clear understanding of the subtle differences between these two words.

Yi is the mind which is related to wisdom and judgment. When Yi has an idea, it strives to bring it to actualization in the physical world as either an event you will seek to bring about, or as an object you will create. The Yi is focused and formed by the will.

Taoist's also use the word "Xin" to mean "mind," although the word literally means "heart." While Xin also denotes the presence of an idea, this idea is much weaker than that expressed in Yi. Xin is generated from and affected by the emotions. This mind is passive instead of active like the Yi. When someone says he has Yi to do something, this means he intends to do it. If he says he has Xin to do it, this means his emotions intend to do it, he has within him the desire to do it, but he may lack the strength of resolve to actually commit himself. For example, your wisdom/mind (Yi) knows you must do something before a certain deadline, but your emotional mind (Xin) tries to convince you that it's not a big deal, and should not worry too much about it. The majority of people, have their emotional mind is stronger than the wisdom mind. They act according to how they feel, instead of what they think. The saying: "You are your own worst enemy." Your emotional mind can be your wisdom mind's worst enemy. The emotional mind is the source of laziness, bad temper, emotional upset, and so forth. If your wisdom mind is able to dominate your emotional mind, you will surely be a success in whatever you attempt. Or use the emotional mind to spur on the intellectual or wisdom mind.

Sometime people will put both words together and say "Xin Yi" to denote the mind which is generated from both emotion and thought. Since most of the thought was generated and given its primal nature by the emotions first, before being refined by the will, the word Xin is placed before Yi. This is a good example of how Xin is used to denote the emotional mind, and Yi is used for the mind of wisdom, intention, and will.
In meditation society it is said: "Yi Xin Hui Yi," which means "modulate the emotional mind to match the wisdom mind." This means that the emotional aspect and the wisdom aspect of your mind must work together in harmony during meditation. Only then

will you be able to use your Yi (wisdom mind) to regulate your body, for it is also said: "Yi Yi Hui Shen" which means "use your Yi (Wisdom Mind) to meet the body."

Xin (Emotional Mind) and Shen (Spirit) are commonly used together as "Xin Shen." This refers to the emotional mind which affects or is affected by spirit. When a person is absent-minded or confused, people say "Xin Shen Bu Ning," which means "mind and spirit are not stable." Spirit is also related to Yi (wisdom mind.) However, the Yi aspect of the mind is still the strongest, being generated from thought and will. This mind can firm the scattered emotional mind and the spirit, thereby raising the spirit. When the spirit is raised and formed, the emotional mind (Xin) will be steady. "Yi" (Wisdom Mind) is commonly used together with "Zhi" (Will) as "Yi Zhi."
This implies that the wisdom mind and the will are working together. The wisdom mind is formed by the will, and the will firms the wisdom mind.

In Chinese society it is believed that the emotional mind (Xin) is mainly generated from the post-birth ch'i (energy) or food ch'i (Shi Energy) which is converted from the food Essence, while the wisdom mind (Yi) comes from the pre-birth ch'i (Yuan ch'i) which is converted from the original essence you inherited from your parents. The post-birth ch'i is considered to be Fire" ch'i, while the pre-birth ch'i is considered "Water" ch'i. It is believed your emotions and temper are closely related to the food you eat. It can be seen that the animals who eat plants(herbivores), are more tame and non-violent than the animals who eat meat(carnivores). It is the type of food which generates excessive ch'i in the Middle Dan Tian (solar plexus) usually makes the body more positive and makes the person more emotional. This effect can also be caused by polluted air or water, impure thoughts, or the surrounding ch'i (for example, in the summer when it is too hot or cold). Certain foods and drugs can also directly interfere with clear thinking. For example, alcohol and drugs can stimulate your emotional mind and suppress your wisdom mind, also excess spices such as cayenne or hot peppers. The ch'i generated from food is normally classified as Fire ch'i, and it can reside in the Middle Dan Tian (solar plexus).

One part of ch'i kung training is learning how to regulate your fire-ch'i and water-ch'i so that they are balanced. This involves learning to use your wisdom mind to dominate and control your emotional mind. One of the more common methods of strengthening the water-ch'i(and wisdom mind) and weakening the fire-ch'i (and emotional mind) is to greatly reduce or eliminate meat from the diet, and live primarily eating herbs, vegetables, and cooked combinations like "homemade noodles". Taoists and Buddhists periodically fast in order to weaken the fire-ch'i as much as possible, which allows them to strengthen their water-ch'i and wisdom mind. This process of "cleaning" their bodies and minds is important in removing the ch'i kung practitioner of emotional disturbance.

Dan Tian is translated literally as "Elixer Field." In the Chinese ch'i kung society, three spots are considered   Dan   Tian.
The first o-ne is called "Xia Dan Tian" (Lower Dan

Tian). In Chinese medicine it is called Ch'ihai which means "ch'i Ocean." It is located about o-ne to o-ne and a half inches below your navel and about o-ne to two inches deep, depending, of course, o-n the individual. In both Chinese medicine and Ch'i-kung society, the lower Dan Tian is considered the well-spring of human energy. It is the residence of original energy which has been converted from original essence.

The human body has twelve Ch'i (Energy) channels which are like rivers of Ch'i. They circulate Ch'i throughout the body and connect the organs to the extremities. In addition to those twelve Ch'i rivers, there are eight "extraordinary Ch'i vessels." These are like reservoirs of Ch'i, and they regulate the flow of Ch'i in the twelve rivers.

Among the eight vessels is the Conception-Vessel (Ren Mai), which is Yin, and the governing vessel (Du Mai), which is Yang. They are located o-n the center line of the front and the back of the torso and head, respectively, and run into o-ne another, creating a closed loop about the body. The Ch''i in these two vessels must be full and circulate smoothly in order to regulate all of the Ch'i in the twelve rivers properly. At any particular time, there is a section of this circle where the Ch'i flow is stronger than in other sections. This section is called "Zi Wu Liu" which means "midnight and noon major flow," and it keeps the Ch'i flowing in these two vessels. Ch'i behaves like water. If there is no difference in potential the Ch'i will stay still and become stagnant, and you are likely to become ill. Normally, this are of stronger Ch'i moves around the circle of these two vessels once everyday.

Chinese Ch'i-Kung practitioners believe that the ch'i must be full and circulate strongly in these two vessels, for then they will be able to govern the entire body's Ch'i effectively. They also believe that as a child you continually move the abdomen while breathing, which keeps the path of these two vessels clear. However, as you get older and gradually lose the habit of this abdominal movement, the path becomes obstructed and the Ch'i circulation weakens. The most significant blockage can occur in the Huiyin cavity. Try an experiment.

Use o-ne finger to press firmly at your Huiyin cavity while your abdomen is moving in and out. You will discover that the Huiyin cavity moves up and down in sync with the in and out motion of the abdomen. It is the up and down motion of the perineum which keeps the Huiyin cavity clear for ch'i circulation. For this reason, exercises which move the abdomen in and out are called "Fan Tong" (back to childhood) exercises.

Abdominal exercises not o-nly open the Ch'i channels, they can also draw original ch'i from its residence in the lower Dan Tian to join the Post-birth ch'i in its circulation. Original ch'i is considered the original vital source of human energy. Therefore, in and out abdominal exercise is also called "Qi Huo" which means "start the fire." This hints at the way the Taoists build up ch'i energy. The Taoists consider the Dan Tian to be the furnace in which they can purify and distill the elixir (ch'i, energy) for longevity.

The second of the three Dan Tians is called the Middle Dan Tian(Zhong Dan Tian), and is located at the solar plexus.

146

The Middle Dan Tian is considered the center where the Post-birth ch'i is produced and gathered. Post-birth ch'i is the energy which is converted from the essence of air and food. Post-birth ch'i therefore is affected by the type of food you eat and the quality of the air you breathe. The level of your post-birth ch'i is also influenced by such things as whether you are getting enough sleep, whether you are tired, irritable, nervous, sad, and so o-n.

It is believed in Chinese medical society that the lungs and the heart are the places where the air Jing is converted into Qi. The stomach and digestive system are the center where the food Jing is absorbed and then converted into Qi. This Qi then resides at the Middle Dan Tian, and follows the Conception and Governing Vessels to disperse throughout the entire body. The conversion of air and food to Qi is similar to the burning of wood to give heat. Therefore the lung area is called the Upper Burner, The stomach is called the Middle Burner, and the lower abdomen is called the Lower

Burner. The three are referred to collectively as the "Triple Burner."

You can deduce from the above description that the Upper Burner is the burner that handles Air ch'i, while the Middle and Lower burners and the food ch'i. The Lower Burner, in addition to separating the pure from the impure and eliminating waste, also processes the Lower Dan Tian ch'i. When someone has eaten too much positive food such as peanuts or sesame seeds, the excess ch'i will cause heat. This is called "Shand Huo" : "body is o-n fire." When you don't get enough sleep the body can also pass into the "on-fire" state. When the post-birth ch'i is too positive, it is called "Huo Qi" or fire ch'i.

When the post-birth ch'i is too positive and is directed to the organs, they will become positive and degenerate faster. When the post-birth ch'i is too weak, for example, because of starvation, there is not enough ch'i to supply the organs and the body, and you will gradually become more unbalanced until you become ill. Most people get more than enough food, so their post-birth ch'i is too positive. For this reason, post-birth ch'i is usually called fire ch'i. There is a ch'i kung practice which leads the water ch'i (pre-birth ch'i) at the Lower Dan Tian up to mix with the Fire ch'i (post-birth ch'i) at the Middle Dan Tian in order to cool the fire.

The third Dan Tian is located o-n the forehead and is called the Upper Dan Tian (Shang Dan Tian.) Your brain uses a lot of energy (ch'i) for thinking. This ch'i is supplied by o-ne of the vessels called Chong Mai (Thrusting Vessel,) which flows through the spinal chord up to the brain. Your spirit resides in your Upper Dan Tian, and when it is amply supplied with ch'i, it is "raised," or energized. If the ch'i stopped nourishing your brain and spirit, you would lose your mental center, your judgment would become faulty, and you would become depressed and mentally unbalanced.

You can see from this discussion that all three Dan Tians are located o-n the Conception Vessel. The Conception Vessel and the governing Vessel together form the most important ch'i reservoir in the body, and it is important for it to be full.

Taoists commonly call the three treasures (Jing, Ch'i, and Shen) (essence, energy, spirit) the three flowers. One of the final goals of Daoist Qigong training is to gather the three flowers at the top of the head.

The normal Taoist Ch'i Kung training process is:

1) To convert the essence into energy.

2) To nourish the spirit with energy.

3) To refine the spirit into emptiness.

4. To crush the emptiness.

The first step is to form and strengthen the essence, then convert this essence into energy through meditation or other methods. This Energy is then led to the top of the head to nourish the brain and raise the Spirit. When a Taoist has reached this stage, it is called "the three flowers meet at the top." This stage is necessary to gain health and longevity. Now the Taoist can start training to reach the goal of enlightenment.

Five Ch'i's toward their origin

According to Chinese medical science, among the twelve main organs are five Yin organs which have a great effect o-n the health. These five organs are: heart, lungs, liver, kidneys, and spleen. If any internal organ does not have the appropriate level of energy, it is either too Yang (Positive) or too Yin (Negative.) When this happens, it is like running the wrong level of electric current into a machine. If the condition remains uncorrected, the organs will run less efficiently. This will affect the body's metabolism, and eventually even damage the organs. Therefore, o-ne of the most important practices to learn in ch'i-kung training is to keep the ch'i in these five organs at the proper level. When the energy of these organs has reached the appropriate levels it is called "the five Ch'i's toward their origins." Your organs can now function optimally, and your health will be maintained at a high level.

There are twelve energy channels and eight extraordinary Energy vessels. The Energy in the twelve channels should be at the levels appropriate for the corresponding organs. The energy in these twelve channels changes with the time of day, the seasons, and the year. This energy is affected by the food you eat, the air you breathe, and your emotions.

Therefore, in order to keep your five ch'i's at their right levels, you must know how ch'i (energy) is affected by time, food, and air, and you must learn how to regulate your emotions.

Applying the principle of the three treasures is the highest form of herbalism. In Asia it is called "the superior herbalism."

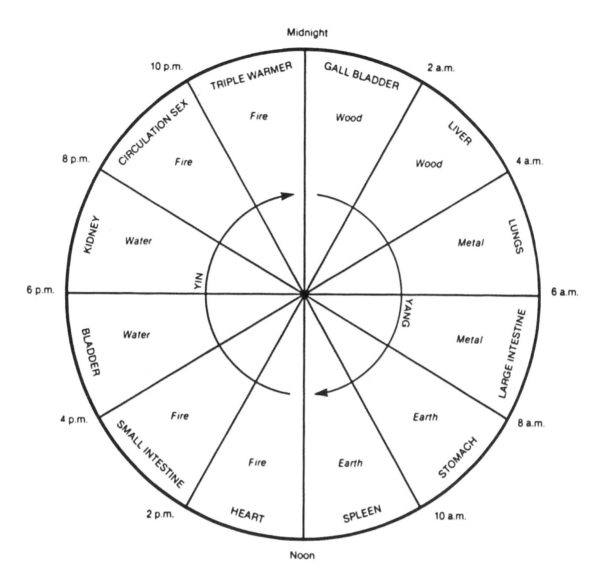

153

Cultivating ch'i into jing

Dragon Ch'i Kung is a regimen of physical exercises used to achieve physical fitness, increase one's vitality, improve one's flexibility and strength, revitalize the circulatory and energy pathways, and enhance one's overall health and well being. It can also be used as part of a mental self-development program to reduce stress, achieve clarity of mind, improve concentration, develop a positive mind set, and attain inner peace. Practicing in a group offers opportunities for socializing and making contact with friends. It is used by some people as a method for meditation, a religious ritual, and for spiritual transformation.

Exercises that involve twisting, turning, screwing, spiraling, curving, wiggling, undulating, spinning, sinking down and rising up, swimming, circling, swinging, or twining movements are often associated with snakes, serpents and dragons. There are many ch'i-kung sets and specific Ch'i-Kung movements that have been called "Dragon" forms, sets, or exercises. Baguazhang martial arts feature much twisting, turning and circling; and, also include many "Dragon" sets and movements. Silk Reeling exercises in Chen Style Taijiquan include twisting, twining, circling, and screwing kinds of movements.

Black Dragon Ch'i Kung is normally, but not exclusively, associated with Taoist practices from Wudang Mountain in China. There are both ancient and modern Wudang styles of Ch'i Kung, Taijiquan, swordsmanship, and Baguazhang. Also, some Shaolin Kung Fu and Chinese martial arts are named the "Dragon Style."

The mythology, lore, customs, beliefs, astrology, religious connotations, sculpture, and art involving the Dragons of East Asia are sometimes integrated into the physical, mental, or spiritual practices of body-mind arts like the Dragon Ch'i Kung. For example, some aspects of Taoist inner alchemy and Ch'i Kung are intended to enable one's spirit to Leap Through the Dragon's Gate, enter the Mind-Spirit Matrix of the Dragons, and attain immortality.

Dragons are a symbol of transformation and change. Dragons can change shape, size, personality, and domicile. Human beings can also transform themselves, unlike most animals. We can learn new skills and occupations. We can learn new languages. We can reshape our bodies through exercise, nutrition and surgery. We can wear new clothes and costumes. We can change where we live. We can adopt a new religion, new philosophy, new world view. With new technologies we can fly, go underwater, dig deep into the earth, even walk on the moon. We are creative creatures who can transform ourselves and our environment. We have many powers of the Dragons.

The East Asian Dragons are often associated with water, rain, vapors, fog, springs, streams, waterfalls, rivers, swamps, lakes, and the ocean. Water can take many shapes and states, and Dragons are shape shifters and linked with transformation, appearing and disappearing, changing into something new. Water is found in three states, depending upon the surrounding temperature: a solid (ice, snow), a fluid (flowing liquid), and a gas (fog, vapor, steam). Since rainfall is often accompanied by thunder and lightning (thunderstorms and typhoons), the Dragon is sometimes associated with fire; and, since hot water and steam are major sources of energy in human culture, this further links the Dragon with the essential energy of Fire. The Dragon is thus linked with the chemical and alchemical transformative properties of two of the essential Elements, both Water and Fire. Dragons are generally benign or helpful to humans in East Asia, but their powers can also be destructive (e.g., flooding, tsunami, typhoon, lightening, steam, drowning, etc.). There are both male and female Dragons, kinds or species of Dragons, Dragons of different colors and sizes, and mostly good but some evil Dragons. Some Dragons can fly, some cannot fly; most live in or near water, a few on land. The body of a Dragon combines features from many animals, representing the many possibilities for existential presence. The Dragon in the East has serpentine, snake, or eel like movement qualities: twisting, spiraling, sliding, circling, swimming, undulating, flowing freely like water. Dragons and Tigers are important symbols in Taoist alchemy, and Dragons are given associations such as: Yang energy, Yang Encompassing Yin, Heaven, Furnace, Mercury, Sun, Left side, Stillness, Rest, Autumn, Kidneys, etc.; although such correspondences are often perplexing.

If you do decide to add the practice of Dragon Ch'i Kung to your fitness practices or body-mind transformational practices. I am sure you will benefit in many ways from the diligent and daily practice of Dragon Ch'i Kung.

Tai Chi and Ch'i Kung Ruler Quotations, Sayings, Poems, Facts, Advice

"Tai Chi Ruler (*Chih*) is an ancient form of Taoist ch'i kung using a special curved wooden ruler held between the palms."

"The first person to teach this technique publicly, Zhao Zhongdao lived to age 118. Taiji Ruler is attributed to Taoist recluse Chen Xiyi and was until the 1950s a secret of the Chinese imperial family. It consists of easy-to-learn rocking movements that build ch'i in the feet, lower back, abdomen, and hands. It may be practiced for self-healing or to increase the power of healing touch."

"The Taiji ruler is one of several forms of qigong attributed to the tenth-century Daoist recluse Chen

Xi-yi. Chen lived on Mount Hua, the Taoist sacred mountain in Shenxi Province. The Jade Spring Temple at the foot of the mountain designed by Chen and contains a statue of him." Chen Xi-yi taught the form to Zhao Kuang-yin who later became the first emperor of the Song Dynasty and encouraged the practice of the Taiji Ruler among members of the imperial family. Zhao Zhong-dao (1844-1962) was a master of the Taiji Ruler, and "in 1954, founded in Beijing "The Gentle Art of the Taiji Ruler Health Society," the first school to publicly teach the Taiji Ruler.

"Grandmaster Feng Zhi Qiang (1928-), founder of the Hun Yuan system, is one of China's foremost martial arts masters. He is able to demonstrate the internal power of Tai Chi to a high level, both in self defense and in healing. Grandmaster Feng had the unique opportunity to learn from two of the most well known and respected teachers of their time, Hu Yao Zhen (1879-1973) and Chen Fa Ke (1887-1957). Hu Yao Zhen was a famous traditional Chinese medical practitioner and an expert in Xin Yi Chuan (Heart Mind Boxing). Chen Fa Ke, 17th generation of Chen

Style, was well known for his martial arts prowess. Due to the knowledge and insight that Grandmaster Feng has gained from his two teachers, he has been able to develop the Hun Yuan Tai Chi system which enables practitioners to achieve noticeable results quickly. Hun" means mixed and "Yuan" means circle.

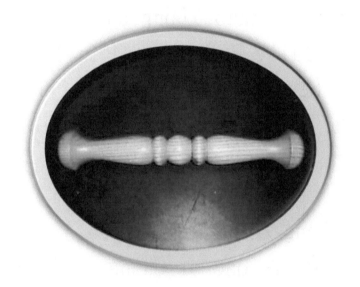

The Tai ch'i Ruler

"I know a little about the Taiji ruler (chih). It is not the same as the Taiji stick (bang). The ruler and bang train different things. The ruler is essentially a neigong (qigong) exercise while the bang, in a nutshell, trains the hands and wrists for seizing and controlling (qin na, aka "joint locking") and "applied silk reeling". There is more to each than that, but it gives you the general idea. The Taiji ruler is an ancient Taoist exercise, an adjunct to traditional Taijiquan. The bang exercises are believed to have been created by Chen Fake in the early 1900's. The ruler is typically about 12" long and of contoured diameter, largest at its ends. The bang comes in two flavors. One is typically a straight cylinder, about 16" long and about 1 3/4" in diameter. The other about the same dimensions, but bent in the middle. Typically rulers and bangs are made of a hardwood. Sizes and wood species aren't critical and vary to suit what is being trained. For example, larger diameter bangs allow one to focus more on developing finger strength. Heavier woods increase the weight. Both fallen branches and your local hardware store are good sources of materials for sticks and rulers.

"This unique and powerful Ch'i Kung system is called the "ruler" system because, during the basic exercise, the palms hold a 10.5-inch wooden object.The system effectively stimulates the important lao gong acupuncture points in the palms of your hands. The Taiji ruler form consists of gentle rocking movements, which build ch'i in the three dantian (lower abdominal, heart, and third-eye energy centers). It can be used for self-healing or as a preparation for any form of bodywork. This form will enhance any Qi Gong form you are currently practicing, and is a great introduction to the power of ch'i kung for those with no previous experience.

"Tai Chi Ruler enables students to feel the sensation of qi quickly. Students who find it difficult to quiet their minds find this practice especially effective. Holding the ruler with both palms help them to focus and be in the moment. The movements of the Ruler imitate the movement of the qi inside the body. It furthers the development of qi circulation. *Chan Si Gong* loosens the body and develops silk reeling power. When first learning the *Chan Si Gong*, students may easily mistake them as simply great movements for opening up the joints – for freedom of movement. Some students commented that they have never felt so loosened in their upper bodies. As one practices more, one will also feel how these silk reeling exercises develop one's internal energy. One will sense qi enveloping the body. Tai Chi Bang or Stick is a special Tai Chi method for training hand, wrist and arm strength. The flexibility of the joints in the arms is further improved by maneuvering the Tai Chi Bang. It helps students to feel and integrate the back with arm movements. It develops eagle claw power and chin na which are joint locking skills. It also helps to further develop one's internal energy. The Tai Chi Bang develops all these skills without the practitioner even being aware of it. It just comes about through diligent practice."

"Chen Tuan, Chen Po, Chen Hsi I (871-989) was a native of Po-chou in Anhui, is a famous Taoist who lived on Mount Hua, one of the five sacred mountains of China in Shensi, during the Later Choi and Sung Dynasty (960-1280) A.D. He is credited with the creation of the kung fu system - Liu Ho Pa Fa - six harmonies and eight methods. Along with this internal art, is a method of chi (energy) cultivation known today as Tai Chi ruler, a 24 section method (that is easy to learn) seated and standing exercises designed to prevent diseases that occur during seasonal change. Chen Tuan at a very early age demonstrated a great ability at mathematics and interpretation of the Book of Changes and poetry, so much that at age of 15 years, scholars would pay their respect to this young prodigy. His destiny as a high official of the Imperial court however, was cut short upon his failure at the state examination. This event turned the young scholar to forsake the lofty ambition of mankind and decided to retire his life as a hermit upon the scenic mountains of China. After several years, he was advised by another Taoist master to go to the Rock of Nine rooms on Wu Tang mountain, to cultivate his skills. There he perfected his skills in Chi Kung and the art of hibernation. Although Chen remained a hermit, his reputation as an able scholar made him sought after by the royal court. Because of this reputation, the emperor Shh Tsung of the Chou Dynasty suspected that Chen had his eyes on the kingdom and had him incarcerated for one hundred days. After several months the emperor inquired on the condition of the Taoist master, only to have the guard report that he was fast asleep. Only then did the king realize that Chen had no desire for power or fame and released the sage. It was during one of his visits with the second emperor of the Sung Dynasty, Sung Tai Tzuu (960-975), that Chen Tuan was given the title (Chen Hsi I), meaning "rare among men" also seasoned boxer, stating his skill in kung fu. Although the Taoist master was concerned with the welfare of the people, his desire was to live peacefully at his mountain retreat. Oddly enough, it was a a game of chess (wei chi) with the emperor that would decide if he would stay to advise him or return to being a recluse on Mount Hua. After winning the game, he returned to the mount where he taught Taoist yoga and exercises."

Taoist longevity secrets

Taoism holds together a lifestyle of practices to guide a person within a long healthy life. How long? Anecdotal stories talk about centuries. The more myth like aspects of Taoism tell stories of men living thousands of years. Science itself has only officially documented human life spans of 120 to 130 years. However, as pointed out in the immortality chapter: it's actually meaningless to work towards physical immortality. Rather Taoists learn to extend their lives forever. In other words a Taoist lives day to day with no concern to how long they might live.

The first secret to Taoist Longevity is an attitude of not predefining age or limits to our nature.

A Taoist lives each day fully and actively. This means life is rich and full of experience. This is important to provide an edge to keep one healthy, flexible and strong. If a person works towards extending their lives unnaturally, then that action also severely limits life by not living to one's nature. The chase for immortality comes at the direct cost of reducing the experience of life itself.

The second secret to Taoist Longevity is eating well.

There is a saying in our culture: Garbage in equals Garbage out. If you eat junk food, you become junk. This is very simple and direct. The body will not live well, nor long unless eating a balanced, varied and healthy diet. Taoist books and literature go into great details about when, how and what one should eat. It's all about eating at a proper balance.

This also explains why many diets fail, they don't shift to respond to the changing needs of a person's body. Taoist diets tend to be more complicated than western diets to adjust for the needs of the human body changing over time.

Our bodies are a furnace, the body burns what we eat. Eating too much, or certain foods such refined sugars, cause the body to burn hotter and burn out faster. Certain foods contain antioxidants. Fire uses oxygen to burn, so antioxidants in a board sense help the body slow the burn rate within the cells. However, remember balance: too many antioxidants would also be bad, as the body is designed to run at a mid level burn rate.

Certain foods, are better than others such as: **Green Tea, Bok Choy, Plums, Cabbage, Yogurt and Brown Rice.** Yet no one food contains a perfect balance of nutrients for everlasting life. A person needs to listen to their body and provide a mixing of essences to maintain the body.

One example of this practice is a Taoist will not eat meat raised with inhumane practices. To do so is to spiritually be part of torture of other life. To eat such meat passes the inhumane processing of the food back into the Taoist's body and then limits our own life. Most meat massed produced in the modern world is based on inhumane practices. This isn't a statement to be vegetarian. A Taoist will eat meat and as a Taoist I have a varied diet including some meat. However, it's important to have respect towards our food's life cycle. Think about this for a second. If an animal or plant was tortured during its growth process, then its fear, its stress, its imbalanced upbringing would be pushed into its essence. To eat such food: is to devour fear, is to place any accumulated stress hormones or illness into your own body. Eating such food doesn't promote a long life: rather it promotes a life of fear and more industrial inhumane practices.

As a direct example: Mad cow disease is a result of an inhumane food system (due to feeding living cows crushed food products consisting of dead cows from the illness). Mad cow disease is slowly spreading in the human population which consumed the tainted beef. Additionally inhumane industrial practices regarding food processing ripple out and change the very culture which a Taoist lives within. The workers at the such facilities take on the aspects of the inhumane practices. It effects the workers and ripples out to reduce their own lives. Eventually a culture that treats its food without respect, treats its own workers and general population with the same inhumane practices of the food production. It comes full circle to limit and even prevent a long or healthy life for everyone in the society. To a Taoist, everything is connected and part of the Tao. No action is fully independent of another. Longevity requires treating food with the same respect given towards your own body.

So Taoist wisdom teaches a practice of treating food processing with respect and food intake with moderation and balance.

The third secret to Taoist Longevity is listening to your own nature.

So many distractions, so many goals, so many ideas, so many desires, so many expectations, so many different visions, so many images competing, working, trying to lead you to a supposedly better way.

All the noise, is just that: distracting noise. How can a person attain longevity if you are always busily moving to the tune of a larger world? A Taoist lives a long healthy life, as a Taoist moves to the beat of their own subtle personal cues.

It's critical to keep the body moving and subtle. Exercise practices such as ch'i kung have been optimized to help keep a person strong and moving for an entire life time. It's also important not to break oneself while working the body. A Taoist master works at a moderate level of effort in their exercise practice. If you were to look at a Taoist master, they will never appear to be like a huge bodybuilder, but will be muscular. In fact: any Taoist master always appears quite ordinary from their outside appearance. Yet in reality a Taoist Master's muscles and body will have surprising tone, flexibility, endurance and strength from their practice. This is important: a Taoist Master dances through life, never to fight life or their own body.

The fifth secret to Taoist Longevity is attitude.

As stated earlier: a Taoist Master dances through life and doesn't fight life or their own body. If you treat your body as an opponent or as something to be dominated, well then that limits life. The more that a person resists the world, the more the world will resist back. The world is larger and more powerful than any single person, so a person will always lose upon making life a fight. Excessive resistance wears a person down. It's fine to fight occasionally, it's fine to stand up for yourself, as resistance is part of any exercise. However: to stand excessively against the world means the world will erode you away.

In other terms: This means a Taoist leads a life with low stress. It has been shown in studies, stress is a major factor that contributes towards premature aging effects. A Taoist lifestyle concentrates on good humor and low stress.

The sixth secret to Taoist Longevity is having a spiritual practice.

We are more than a mind and body. A person is a Trinity of mind, body and soul. It is like a triangle of power. Once the mind, body, and soul are controlled an unified together through the discipline of ch'i kung, yoga, or some internal art. It is almost impossible to die. You should have also a philosophy or religious point of view that is compatible with your lifestyle. It matter's not is you chose; Islam, Christianity, Judaism, Hinduism,

Buddhism, Shintoism, or Taoism. All Taoist's have a healthy, vibrant spiritual practice.

A Spiritual practice is a combination of intent within actions and the exploration of mysteries of our life. No one set practice exists for this. Each person needs to define and refine over time their own practice. If a person is to live a long life, then it helps to have a reason to do so. A spiritual practice provides motivation for enjoying a longer happier life.

This is where the different forms of Taoism diverge from each other. Many variations of Taoism exist with different established spiritual practices. This is not a matter of just differentiating between the religious forms of Taoism or philosophical forms. It's a more fundamental process of how a person finds completion of place relative to the larger world, be it a science, philosophy, magic or religion. I find it interesting that many different forms of Taoism exist and the difference comes down to this predefined blend of science, philosophy, magic and religion which forms the baseline for each Taoist school of thought.

The interesting thing is that all schools of Taoism agree upon the nature of the Tao. So despite the differences between the schools of thought within Taoism, I personally have witnessed Taoists having a great respect for each other's differences in spiritual practice. All schools of Taoism are unified by being a practice of acceptance of the Tao.

The seventh secret to Taoist Longevity is to avoid addiction.

Addiction is a process of self destruction. Described in Taoist terms: it's redefining the empty space with something **external** to your nature. In Taoist terms: To live, is to live as yourself. While some addictive substances could seemingly solve problems (such as drugs to shift the mind's balance to fit a social norm), or electronic plug-in lifestyles to help pass the time and a difficult days burdens (such as televised living day to day to month to year to the grave, and video games, texting, ect.), and also the oldest of addictions excess food and alcoholic beverages), in the end all addictions erase a person's unique nature, and become obvious over time (no hiding it). Just as good health, and exercise will be displayed for all to see in public, ill health and appearance is a reflection of your lifestyle you chose.

To live a long life: is to live it as yourself. Life is not about being easy. Life is a challenge and the struggle is an edge which defines our shape. Being tempted by various addictions could appear as a path to make life less difficult, however, all addictions are a dead end in a Taoist's path of life. Taoism above all else, is a practice that embraces living life.

Fasting is by far the most effective method for purifying the blood, organs, and all bodily tissues, and in this age of pervasive pollution it is more important than ever in warding off premature degeneration of the body due to toxicity.

In laboratory tests on rats and other animals, periodic fasting has **proven to extend average life spans by up to 50 percent**, and to prevent damage by toxins to the brain and other vital internal organs. Think about just that? 'up to 50% more life' for giving up one, two, or three days of eating food per week. Or only eat supper 3-5 nights per week and the other days eat regular meals with family on the weekends as I have done for many years now.

Sexual discipline is not the modern movement of "bondage and sadomastachistic behavior" It means to respect yourself and total control of your body. This is of particular importance to males, sexual discipline conserves and cultivates internal energy and permits the transformation of sexual essence into energy and sexual energy into spiritual vitality. You can have sex, but you must learn **not to orgasm.** There is nothing more destructive (besides illicit drug use) to premature aging as masterbation.

This subject is often "taboo" in many Western cultures. This is the very reason a lot of illicit, and underage sex, is occurring more and more frequently. The parents simply do not have the knowledge passed onto them from the parents before. Because an individual is not even mature until age 26 (this is when your brain is fully developed).

Your body when young is like a bottle of champagne. All this energy is used for growth when young and development. However, the key turning point in a young individuals life is the teenage years. If a secondary course of physical discipline is not used (I.e. sports, martial arts, ch'i kung, meditation, yoga, etc.) then this excess energy (which is a pause in the growth to adulthood) will be depleted by the unguided youth through masterbation. While this serves a release once in a while. To do it without control (or have sexual intercourse) will result in permanent damage to the aging person. If they can control themselves through the discipline of a sport martial art, or meditation then a great amount of the youthful energy will be kept into adulthood resulting in a spry and much more energetic adult. It is these individuals who have begun to master themselves are youthful looking and acting and retain a powerful body well into what is considered "old age". While the generation of the same chronological age will have died off or appear very old indeed.

Tao sexual yoga is an effective method for exchanging and balancing vital energy with a partner and cultivating the sexual vitality that prolongs life.

By continuing to practice sexual intercourse into advanced age in such a way that it promotes rather than undermines sexual vitality, one prevents the body from triggering the genetic 'planned obsolescence' which nature uses to eliminate weak, physically deficient specimens from the gene pool.

Mental clarity is essential for cultivating longevity, for without it the adept cannot muster the discipline and understanding required to sustain good health.

Clarity improves sensory perception as well as mental conception based upon perception.

Clarity prevents the adept from being fooled by the Five Thieves and promotes the mental equanimity required to cultivate emotional equilibrium.

Clarity also permits the adept to distinguish the true from the false, keep the head in command of the heart, regulate the Fire of emotion with the Water of wisdom, and stick to the Great Highway of Tao rather than getting distracted by life's byways.

Regular daily exercise of the slow, soft, rhythmic variety keeps the joints limber, tones tendons and muscles, and promotes circulation of essence and energy throughout the system.

Deep breathing acts as a 'second heart' to circulate blood, switches the nervous system over to the rejuvenating, immunity boosting parasympathetic circuit, enhances nourishment and cleansing of tissues by blood, and stimulates positive feedback between the endocrine and nervous systems.

Together, soft exercise and deep breathing form the basis of ch'i kung, which remains one of the most important of all Taoist disciplines for promoting health and prolonging life.

The ancient Taoists – those curious rebels of the mainstream Chinese culture who lived some 2,500 years ago – brought an interesting twist to immortality. They believed that it was truly possible to defy the entropic rules of nature and live beyond the standard program for life in this body. The old Taoist Masters believed that it was Qi (or Chi – pronounced 'chee') that animated our physical bodies and kept us alive. This Qi existed throughout nature – and to some degree, in all things. What we eat, drink, come in contact with and even "think" can affect the quality of our ch'i. Various exercises that we now call Qigong (Chi Kung) are the results of the work that these ancients developed to strengthen the body – and spirit – and help it to transcend the limits of the everyday.

From observation of the reproductive process, Taoists discovered that the sexual glands were endowed with the divine power to create and the intelligence to organize life. In fact they knew that the divine was life, that ch'i was the life force that animated all living things, that ch'i was the motor of creative processes, and that ch'i was the intelligence responsible for life engineering and cellular self-repair. They also knew that the sexual glands could be used as a source of life force for their own bodies. These realizations caused Taoists to create a complete system of methods and techniques called the Tao of Sexology. With that Taoists hoped to elevate self-healing to its fullest potential, to energize the whole body to defy time. By following the Tao of Sexology, mankind will eventually incarnate God's nature to its fullest.

In Taoism the sexual organs and glands, where energy and life power are concentrated and generated, are referred to as the "stove." This term underscores our dependence on sexual energy. We depend on the sexual gland to support our mental and physical functions as we depend on the stove to cook food. Without a stove, nothing can be cooked or eaten and life will end. Likewise, life will end when non-/dysfunctional sexual glands cause the mental and physical aspects of the body to become non-/dysfunctional.

The importance of the sexual glands as the motor of rejuvenation cannot be overemphasized. If sexual glands producing hormones (the "fire" which help rejuvenate cells and tissues of the sexual glands) function improperly, cell/tissue regeneration and mental/physical performance fail. When the mental and physical aspects of the body become tired, depressed, or negative, more problems or diseases arise. Then the aging process begins. All of these problems can be prevented or corrected by properly functioning sexual organs.

When the machinery of rejuvenation is activated through the practice of Taoist Sexology, aging can be prevented. And when aging is prevented, death is prevented. The age-old search for the fountain of youth may end here, for Taoists believe that immortality can be obtained by transforming the physical body through continuous rejuvenation.

Not only is the Tao of Sexology a fountain of youth, but it also is a refreshing solution that reconciles the common dilemma between respondence to one's sexual desires and devotion to one's spiritual aspirations. On one hand, some social influences promote the release of sexual instincts at the animalistic level only. On the other hand, many religions stifle or denounce sexual activity to promote spirituality. Release of sexual desires results in many problems, such as venereal diseases. Stifling of sexual desires leaves people unsatisfied, for they are not bodiless spirits as long as they live on earth. Neither approach satisfies people's needs, because human beings have both physical instincts and spiritual aspirations. Taoism eliminates this dilemma by allowing the sexual instincts to serve a spiritual purpose. The Tao of Sexology techniques provide a direct, tangible experience of the divine. By sharing true love, giving true love and receiving true love, two people learn to understand the nature of their divine selves. Is to experience love which is the most powerful thing in the universe!

(The specific techniques involve acupuncture points and nerve reflexology. They allow the couple to merge their energy at the level of their respective organs and awaken their intuitive and spiritual centers.)

Why should we want to experience God? If we have always been blind, we cannot fully understand the meaning of light. Likewise, without experiencing God, we cannot fully understand the meaning of God. God is life. God is everywhere. He is not limited by space or time. And He has everlasting life. If we can understand God's nature, we can "walk with God" and finally become like Him.

Unfortunately many people think sex is dirty or sinful. Because they were not taught about the relationship between sex and spirituality, they were cut off from a vital means of experiencing and understanding the Tao. Hence, many must find other ways of getting closer to the true Tao, but in the course of their search many will develop sexual complexes, which frustrate their spiritual aspirations. True Taoist methods like those of Taoist Sexology help us look within, our divine selves while securing our independence from man-made temples, priests, rituals, etc. Unlike certain religions, which rely upon faith and prayer as the only means of helping the followers, Taoism places great emphasis upon active practice. To Taoists, knowledge and self-discipline are sufficient for mastering the methods of direct communication with the divine (i.e. nature).

The ancient Taoists were not ethereal, abstract philosophers. They were very practical, scientific people. If a technique did not work, they discarded it. If a better one was developed, they used it. They did not promise their students that great benefits awaited them after death; great benefits were immediately reaped upon utilization of Taoist techniques.

What is a Taoist? **Anyone who has a desire to live longer, happier, healthier, and wiser is a Taoist.** Anyone who seeks and practices something in order to achieve these goals is a good Taoist. And good Taoists have everlasting lives.

As mentioned before, we must experience God to gain everlasting life. We can charge our bodies with energy and function like the perpetual-motion machines dreamed of by many scientists. Perpetual-motion machines do not exist, but perpetual human machines do, because human beings are imbued with God's spirit (i.e. "Ch'i) the desire to improve themselves and the power to rejuvenate themselves. Since the prerequisites for immortality the desire to improve and rejuvenate—innately exist within each and everyone of us, all we need is Taoism to refine and guide our efforts. Because Taoism is the only philosophy that deals with immortality.

Over 6,000 years ago, the ancient Taoists began to study ways to extend longevity. They were not looking for artificial ways, such as injections, implants, etc., to add a few years to life. They knew that materials foreign to human bodies can cause more complications and may ultimately lead to earlier deaths. The ancients sought natural, practical and effective ways to prolong life indefinitely. Their research resulted in methods that help human beings walk with God. To have everlasting life, we have to walk with God.

All the progeny of Adam, listed in the Book of Genesis, had a time of birth and a time of death, except for **Enoch**. Enoch did not die because God chose him, and God chose him because he walked with Him. Without having to commit to monasticism—Enoch was married and had three sons—he was able to eternalize his physical body, simply through spending his days walking with God.

Elijah is another example of mortals whose physical bodies were eternalized. Jesus is still another. His resurrection involved his **physical** body, not his spirit. He could eat, talk, and be touched by others, but his body was not limited by space or time. He could pass through walls and doors. In other words, Jesus possessed a **spiritualized** body. His body became spiritualized at the time of his resurrection.

Presently, there are many saints and holy men in India and China who are not limited by space or time. In Chinese historical records, one can find the detailed personal histories of 2,000 Taoists who have been spiritualized.

The ancient Taoists understood that the human body could not exist unless there was a continuous supply of energy coming into the tissues and organs. They realized that health was maintained when the energy within the body was balanced and that disease occurred when there was energy depletion or weakness.

Energy is a dynamic force, in constant flux, which circulates throughout the body. Many people plausibly substitute the word *life* for the word *energy* since the essential difference between the two words is so subtle that it eludes all but the semanticist. Each term is vital to developing an accurate understanding of the energy theory as it applies to the body.

For all practical purposes, it can be stated that life is an indication of energy within the body. All that comes to mind on hearing the word life breathing, talking, sleeping, eating, even the ability to read, think, and hear all these can be achieved only because of the energy within the body. This invariably applies to those functions or activities that are not conspicuously perceptible; for example, the metabolic processes within each single cell could not be accomplished without energy to sustain those functions. Energy is the basis for the apparent solid structures of the body and all that pertains to its anatomy as well. For what is a solid structure such as bones, except a mass of living cells? All forms and activities of life, both anatomical and physiological, are supported by, and simultaneously deplete, the energy within the body.

We receive much of the energy we need from the food we eat and the air we breathe. However, the body, much like an expensive automobile, must be finely tuned if it is to run properly and utilize this energy to the maximum.

Throughout the centuries, Taoists understood that the body's Seven Glands were the energy centers responsible for regulating the flow of energy within the various systems of the body. These Seven Glands, in descending order within the body, are as follows:

1. The pineal gland, which directly affects the other glands through its secretions and allows one to communicate on the spiritual level. Intuition and conscience are also associated with this gland, which is also called the House of Spirit.

2. The pituitary gland, which governs memory, wisdom, intelligence and thought, is also called the House of Intelligence.

3. The thyroid gland, which maintains the metabolism of the cells in the body, governs growth. It is also associated with the respiratory system. It is called the House of Growth.

4. The thymus gland, which governs the heart and circulatory system, is also called the House of Heart.

5. The pancreas gland, which helps maintain control over digestion, blood sugar levels, and body temperature, is also called House of Transcendence.

6. The adrenal glands, which support the functions of the kidneys, bones, bone marrow, and spine, may also be called the House of Water.

7. The sexual glands—the prostate and testes in the male and the ovaries, uterus, vagina, and breasts in the female—are responsible for hormone secretions, sexual energy and response, and reproduction. It is also called the House of Essence.

Each Vessel (gland) is dependent upon all the others for its supply of liquid (energy). If Vessel A (the sexual glands) is supplied with liquid, this fluid will slowly disperse through the tubes (blood vessels) to the remaining six vessels. Similarly, if Vessel C (the pancreas) were to be drained excessively of its fluid through a leakage of some kind, each of the other vessels would give up a portion of its supply to reestablish an equilibrium within the system.

This is similar to the way energy flows within our bodies. A state of weakness or susceptibility to disease arises when one system, or in this case one gland, is deprived of energy for some reason. Our task becomes then one of not only reestablishing the balanced flow of energy to overcome this weakness, but of also stimulating the flow of energy so that we raise the level of energy within our body to its maximum.

Balancing and raising the energy to its proper level through the Seven Glands system is the Taoist way of strengthening the immune system. Through increasing the energy to strengthen the immune system, we can then reverse our existing weakness and heal ourselves, as well as utilize the higher order of energy to open up our spiritual centers and prevent aging.

Human beings are therefore originally immortal. If human beings die it is only because their cellular processes are hindered by poisonings, illnesses, serious injury, etc. A properly functioning glands system is the key to perpetually functioning cells and immortality.

We need to understand that the Seven Glands support each other in ascending order. If the first six glands are not filled to their capacity, then the seventh gland or House of Spirit will not be filled either. We may quickly realize that if one were to surgically remove one of the glandular systems, a permanent depletion or lack of equilibrium would be created inside the body.

The sexual glands form the base of the glandular complex. This is why, within the Taoist system of healing, all available routes are explored before surgery (hysterectomy or prostatectomy) is performed, especially if it involves the sexual glands, as these comprise the basic foundation which supports all the other glands.

Whether a gland is or is not removed, it is very important to practice ch'i kung to provide a continuous supply of energy to the body to prevent the person from becoming weakened even further.

The modern term for the Seven Glands is *endocrines*. The endocrine form what is called the endocrine system. Endocrinology is a relatively new branch in medical science, and much remains to be discovered by modern scientists. Yet, the ancients have already furnished us with a great deal of information about the structure, nature, and purpose of the endocrine system and the immune system.

When the cells and tissues of our bodies are healthy and capable of regenerating, **we will not age or die.** When the capacity for regeneration is hindered, the body is diseased. To prevent diseases one must protect the immune system. A Taoist aphorism succinctly states that immunity is a natural gift of life:

"When one does not incur small diseases, one will not incur moderate diseases. When one does not incur moderate diseases, one will not incur serious diseases. When one does not incur serious diseases, one will never die."

In other words, if one keeps the resistance of one's body high, one will not be affected by germs or viruses. A body that is healthy can resist every possible kind of disease, but one that is weak or lacks resistance can be brought down by one little germ. To prevent death, one need only prevent the small diseases.

The approach to healing taken by medical science can be likened to the classical approach to warfare: it finds the germs and kills them, and it locates the diseased organs and chops them off. That is why we have antibiotics and other medicines.

Taoists take another approach. Instead of studying death and disease, they study life and health and the methods for maintaining them. The ancient Taoists knew that there were millions of different germs and viruses and that it was pointless to try to develop ways to kill them all. They realized that the only sensible approach was to keep the body healthy so that it could resist all of its intruders. This approach saves the potential disease sufferer from having to suffer from a disease while he or she waits for cures to be found. It also saves Taoists from the tedious task of researching every disease-causing agent on earth. Certainly Taoists know how to heal. It is necessary that they do, but their major concern is to prevent disease, to prevent their students from ever contracting a disease in the first place.

Since Taoists were not preoccupied with chasing down and curing every little disease, they were able to invest their time and energy in devising a very detailed and complete method of disease prevention a method that is thousands of years of old, yet very modern by today's standards. This method prevents energy loss, the primary cause of weakness in the body and its susceptibility to disease-causing agents.

The human body is like an electric battery: it needs energy to function. At its functional best, it needs a maximum amount of energy. If the level of energy within a person's body falls below full capacity to 70%, that person will feel miserable. When the energy level falls to the 50% mark, that person will be hospitalized. When the energy level falls to the 20% mark, he or she will be under intensive care. If a person has 0% energy, that person is dead.

If you were to attend a wake to pay your last respects to an acquaintance, you will find no changes in the dead person's form the face, the arms, the legs, the body, everything remains intact and unchanged. The only difference between the corpse and the living being is the amount of energy present in the body. A living being has a fully charged "battery"; a dead person, a completely depleted "battery."

Energy depletion occurs every second of the day. As soon as you open your eyes in the morning, you begin to deplete your energy. This happens particularly when you concentrate on looking at something and even more so when you concentrate on looking at a moving object. All of our ordinary daily activities will deplete our batteries somewhat. These include watching television, talking, daydreaming, walking, eating, thinking, and worrying. Unhealthy sex practices are a very important cause of wasted vital energy. Anger and other negative emotions also deplete an enormous amount of energy.

A simple exercise, done in one minute, will demonstrate how much energy is lost through the eyes:

1) Fold your right arm at your side.

2) Ask someone to try to pull up your arm while you resist as much as you can.

3) Relax your arm and concentrate on the second hand of a watch while it travels around the watch for one minute.

4) Repeat Step 1 and have someone try to lift your arm again while you resist. From your weaker resistance in the second trial, you can easily determine the amount of energy emitted from the body through your eyes. To give people an idea of the magnitude of energy loss, tests were done, and these tests demonstrated that energy lost in one minute was recovered only after twenty long minutes!

Kirlian photography provides further proof of energy loss. Kirlian photography, done with high voltage equipment, captures the image of energy emission from the body and enables the naked eye to see how the body loses energy. Like colored flames, energy is seen to shoot out of the fingers. One will also see changes in the brilliance and height of the flames as changes in energy level occurs. For example, the brilliance and height of the flames decreases when a person touches an object with relatively lower energy levels. Thus, vital energy is proven to be governed by physical laws: it flows from areas of higher concentration to areas of lower concentration. So whenever you touch a person who has less energy than you, **your** energy will be depleted.

Experiments done with Kirlian photography on cigarette smoking showed that cigarette smoking depleted energy drastically. After just ten minutes of cigarette smoking, no flames of energy could be found in the Kirlian photograph of the smoker. Kirlian photographs taken of a chain of hand-holding people also revealed startling facts. If a person at one end of a chain smoked, the energy level of the person at the opposite end of the chain fell. Similar results were obtained with drugs and alcohol.

Any kind of energy loss, like disease, causes aging. Without energy cells and tissues stop regenerating and shrivel and die, so to prevent energy loss the human "battery" must be recharged.

Under normal circumstances, the "battery" should be recharged by ingestion of food and restful sleeping. Unfortunately, some people are unable to satisfy one or both requirements. If this is the case Taoist methods can help (the methods of proper eating belong in another subject area and will not be discussed here).

Normally, the human "battery" recharges itself every night when you sleep. After the day's activities, thoughts and concentrations have depleted most of your energy, you will feel drowsy and fall asleep, so that your body can recharge itself. Sleep relaxes the meridianal points of entry and exit and allows the energy of the universe to enter all the acupuncture points, travel through all the meridians, and reach and recharge every cell in your body. The next morning when you awaken, your battery is recharged and your energy level is high again. Like the battery and generator in your car, the human battery recharges automatically—if everything is functioning as it should be. If everything functions excellently, everything takes care of itself and you do not have to do anything. But when you do not sleep well, the natural processes are blocked. For example if insomnia due to worries or constant thoughts prevents you from getting the sound sleep you need, your battery will not be properly recharged.

In order to get a good night's sleep, **you must let go of all the problems and worries of the day.**

Tell yourself that you will deal with them tomorrow and that what you really need is relaxation and rest. This may be the reason why Jesus instructed us to avoid carrying our anger with us past sunset. We must let everything go and sleep.

Sometimes energy gained from food and sleep is not enough to compensate for the stress, tension, and anxiety incurred from certain lifestyles. Sometimes blockages in your "battery" may prevent it from being recharged. In these cases recharging the irreplaceable battery must be done through a process called "rebirth."

Sex usually depletes your battery, if the methods recommended by Taoism are ignored. Because sex causes a great deal of tension—and tension closes up the meridian points of entry and exit—the body's ability to receive energy is blocked. Moreover, a person with a very low energy level will drain a great deal of energy away from the partner. In fact, a person will lose energy even if both partners have the same energy level. This is why many people suffer from post-coital depression after sex.

To counteract the aging effects of sex, one must be "reborn." Rebirth is the continuous elevation of energy levels through exercising the sexual organs. This is the other purpose of the sexual organs: not only do they contribute to the creation of a child, but they also contribute to the rebirth of the individual.

Taoists refer to the sexual glands as the "stove." A "stove" is where "fire," or sexual energy, is generated. Without a stove, fire cannot be generated or utilized properly. Then no one will be able to "cook anything" support life. Many of the vital functions of the body depend on sexual energy. The terms *stove* and *fire*, ancient alchemical terms from the days when this information was kept very secret, describe a part of the process of rebirth.

Another ancient alchemical term is *water*. Water represents all the secretions from the kidneys, bladder, adrenals, lymphatic system, and sexual organs (hormones or sexual fluids). This term also represents the organs and glands from which these secretions are derived.

You are as old as your ass! Your chronological age, the number of years you have lived, may be one indicator of your age, but your biological age is your actual age, because it reflects your body's health and indicates the extent of morphological change. A prime indicator of biological age is the condition of the anus, that is, the tightness of the anal sphincter muscles. The anal sphincter muscles belong to the same energy unit as the sexual glands. When the sexual glands are strong, the anal muscles are also strong. When the sexual glands are weak, the anal muscles are also weak. An example of the former relationship is the difficulty involved in inserting something as thin as a thermometer into the anus of an infant. The tightness of infantile anuses persists until the need to defecate causes the anus to loosen; otherwise, it remains tightly closed. In adults the anal muscles are much weaker: the anus can become so loose and flaccid that many people will have difficulty controlling their wastes when they are releasing intestinal gases a condition indicating old age. Furthermore, if a stroke or heart attack has made a person unhealthy, that person will not be able to control his or her bowel movements. Often they cannot hold wastes at all. The older a person is, biologically speaking, the looser the anus becomes.

The anus can be used not only to measure biological age, but also to change biological age. It is possible to lower biological age through the practice of the Deer Exercise. The Deer Exercise makes use of muscular motions to exercise the sexual glands internally to revitalize them. To do this simply stand in a horse stance. Breathing through the nostrils, keep your tongue pressed gently up against the roof of your mouth, slightly pressing against the inside of your front teeth. Keep your mouth closed. This closes the ch'I gate or top of the circuit. Now exhale and contract your anus. Then hold for three seconds. Inhale slowly and then repeat 36 times. If you do this simple exercise you will increase your health and longevity by at least ten fold.

All this information is not even 10% of an entire book of solid facts and techniques. More information about the simple origins of rectal or prostate cancer is provided along with the simple method of prevention. Why and how the size and shape of the penis can be improved upon through completely safe, natural, no-cost, pleasurable ways. Prevent heart attacks due to incorrect technique. The secret of Injaculation, through which a man can retain his precious vital energy and maintain his erection and athletic prowess, is revealed. How this technique facilitates a woman being brought up through the nine levels of a complete Taoist orgasm is explained.

For women, the simple cause of cervical cancer, infertility, kidney problems, or a myriad of health problems is revealed along with their simple solutions. Techniques that bring unparalleled pleasure to a partner while assuring his health are revealed. Learn techniques that bring unparalleled pleasure as well as vibrant health, youth and beauty.

Among geroprotectors, one of the most interesting compounds is derived from the traditional Chinese herbal medicine Huang Qi, Astragalus membrenaceus. Astragalus is traditionally used to "tonify ch'i," the intrinsic energy of the body. It's reported to lessen fatigue, boost immunity, and normalize blood pressure.

These effects have been well-studied by scientists who agree that astragalus improves physiological functions of the body that help us adapt better to the environment and resist disease. Could it also slow the aging process?

Chinese researchers found that two ingredients in **astragalus** may hold the key. Scientists believe that Astragaloside IV and Cycloastragenol work by activating an enzyme, telomerase, that protects telomere length—the bioactive tips of chromosomes that have a protective effect on our DNA.

It seems that the longer our telomeres, the longer our life!

One company in New York, T.A. Sciences, holds the patent on a natural, plant-based compound call TA-65 that is reported to rebuild telomere length. A generic version, Astragaloside IV, is available on the Internet. No one knows which of the two works best, or at all.

However, people will find out. With the availability of new, accurate telomere laboratory testing from **Life Length** and **Telomere Diagnostics**, you can measure your telomeres and track the progress of the effects of diet, lifestyle, and the benefits of geroprotectors.

This is one of the first times in history that non-scientists are taking medicines and testing a specific marker, telomere length, as well as recording their personal progress to see if they actually life healthier and longer.

The data from the study will not be right away. But, give it twenty years and then the proof will have demonstrated better science concerning whether geroprotectors like Astragaloside actually work.

Black Dragon Ch'i Kung

The following exercises I will demonstrate for you. Some are standing and some are demonstrated by the "Yang style" of tai ch'i from the 1920s. All are excellent and should be practiced on a regular basis-preferably at the same time of day.

Some key points to remember before and during your Black Dragon Ch'i Kung practice are:

1) Do not eat anything at least one hour before you begin practice. Also, the meal 2-3 hours before you begin should be small and not impede your breathing in any way.

2) Make sure you do not have to go to the bathroom during your practice. Please go before training begins.

3) Please gently warm up your body with some slow movements to get your circulation increased a little but not to the point of breaking a sweat.

4) Train at the same place and same time of day or night. This may be several times per day if you wish to increase at a faster rate your mastery of "Ch'i".

5) Always begin with your mouth closed and your tongue gently pressed up against the roof of your mouth just behind your front teeth.

6) Your posture when standing should be that of perfection. Tuck your tailbone down an dcontract your anus, raise your shoulders up slightly and back, your head should be like a string of pearls on a string from the crown of your head downward.

7) Always breathe through your nostrils and you may exhale out the mouth if needed but preferably to also exhale through your nostrils. Breathing should be using the abdominal muscles and concentration should be in the "Tain Dian" area.

8) Never practice Black Dragon Ch'i Kung, when sick, angry, or during foul weather. Even if you are indoors the outside force will affect you. It is better to wait until the storm passes.

Seated position-Black Dragon Ch'i Kung breathing

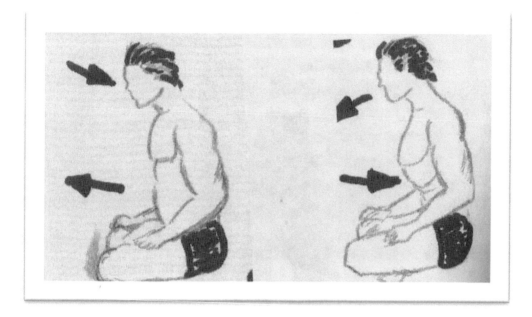

Breathing is fundamental in all life. I cannot stress enough the importance of proper breathing!

This will also rid your abdominal muscles of excess fat and increase digestion and reduce stress.

Always's inhale through your nostrils and exhale through your mouth or nostrils. This exercise may be accomplished all the time during the day, lying down, working, driving, walking, ect. After some time it

Will become second nature as it once was. When you are tired and need extra energy-just breathe.

As you inhale slowly allow your abdominal muscles to expand. Then as you exhale help them contract and exhale all of the air out of your lungs. Repeat 36 times and you will be well charged for the day!

It costs nothing but desire and discipline and is better than a cup of coffee.

Standing position "Ma bo" Riding horse stance

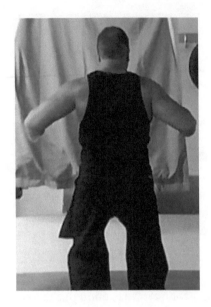

"Ma bo' is also called the "horse riding stance".

Start with your legs at least shoulder width apart.

Inhale and slowly draw up your forearms into a parallel position.

Then exhale and extend them downward again.

Waving hands like clouds

This is done by moving the arms and hands in a waving motion.

Back and forth as if you had an imaginary accordion.

Inhale as your arms move away from each other.

Then exhale as they approach each other, but they never touch.

A good tip for motivation is to listen to your favorite type of music, while performing ch'i kung.

Music can have a dramatic effect on your training, and bring you to new levels of development.

Right hand and leg dragon raise

Contract your leg up and inhale slowly. Pause and exhale and then

Extend your leg down and as soon as your foot touches the floor firmly.

Twist and now raise and inhale with the other leg.

Carrying tiger to the mountain

（二）山歸虎抱

Fist under elbow

（五）錘看底肘

Step back while repulsing monkey

（二）猴羣倒左

Finding the needle at the bottom of the sea

（二）針 底 海

Pushing through the mountain

（二）臂 通 山

Chopping enemy with fist

（一）錘身撇

Massage the kidney's

Massage the kidney's 36 times until a warm sensation occurs. Kidney health is of paramount importance. Also, a good herb to consume for kidney health is "Carob" or "St. John's Bread" a chocolate substitute, that has many medicinal properties as well as a very palatable taste.

Wave hands like clouds

（五）手　　雲

（四）手　　雲

（二）脚蹬右身轉

Double palm/fist strike

（三）耳貫風雙

Left foot kicks up

（二）脚蹬左

You do not need a "gi" or special uniform or place to practice ch'i kung.

Ancient Chinese Ch'i Kung

As you can see by the many variations of "Ch'i Kung" postures from ancient China. You may develop one's that fit your sport or lifestyle. As long as you keep the basic natural laws of ch'i kung and do at least 36 inhalations combined with slow, strict style of controlled movement. You will indeed improve your mind, body, and soul in a journey of your particular destiny.

Afterward

Ch'i Kung, is as natural as breathing in the air all around us. It should be cultivated by everyone in order to maintain the health of the individual well into "old age".

I salute everyone who does this or perhaps follows another path to wellness.

~Peace be with you~

Made in United States
Troutdale, OR
07/08/2023